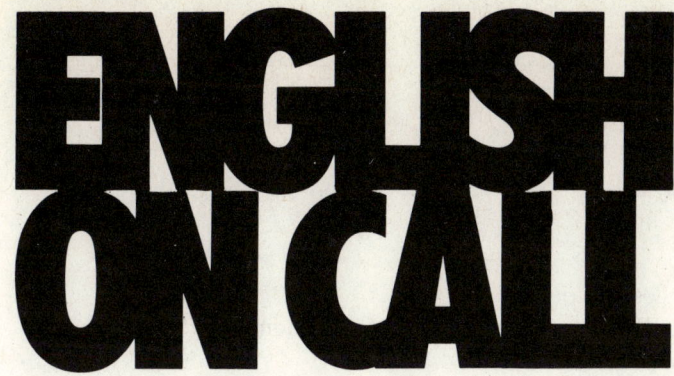

LEVEL ONE

Victoria F. Kimbrough

Marjorie Vai

McGRAW–HILL, INC.

New York St. Louis San Francisco Auckland Bogotá
Caracas Hamburg Lisbon London Madrid Mexico
Milan Montreal New Delhi Paris San Juan
São Paulo Singapore Sydney Tokyo Toronto

Editorial Development
Project Editor: Karen Davy

Book Production
Art Direction and Design: Leslie Nolan
Illustrators: James Hoston, Barbara Lehman, Susan Greenstein
Cover Illustration: Barbara Lehman
Typography: Onno de Jong

Photographs:
pg. 12: courtesy The Biltmore Hotel
pg. 18: both: UPI/Bettmann Newsphotos
pg. 26: © Roy Attaway/Photo Researchers
pg. 32: left to right: UPI/Bettmann Newsphotos; Alexander Lowry/Photo Researchers; © G.T. Hillman/Photo Researchers; UPI/Bettmann Newsphotos; AP/Wide World Photos
pg. 36: Left column, top: © Hal Harrison/Photo Researchers
middle: © Jerome Wexler/Photo Researchers
bottom: © Bettye Lane/Photo Researchers
Right column, top: © Arvind Garg/Photo Researchers
middle: © Ylla/Photo Researchers
bottom: © Jane Latta/Photo Researchers
pg. 43: all 6: UPI/Bettmann Newsphotos
pg. 64: UPI/Bettmann Newsphotos
pg. 96: © Bill Bachman/Photo Researchers

Copyright © 1991 by McGraw-Hill, Inc. All rights reserved. Printed in the United States of America. Except as permitted under the United States Copyright Act of 1976, no part of this publication may be reproduced or distributed in any form or by any means, or stored in a database or retrieval system, without the prior written permission of the publisher.

Contents

Introduction　　　　　　　　　　　　　*v*

Unit 1　　　　　　　　　　　　　　　　*1*
Subject pronouns
This and *that*
To be – Simple present

Unit 2　　　　　　　　　　　　　　　　*8*
There is and *there are*

Unit 3　　　　　　　　　　　　　　　　*15*
WH- questions with *to be*

Unit 4　　　　　　　　　　　　　　　　*21*
Possessive adjectives

Unit 5　　　　　　　　　　　　　　　　*27*
Simple present tense:
　affirmative, interrogative,
　short answers

Unit 6　　　　　　　　　　　　　　　　*36*
Simple present tense:
　WH- questions, negative

Unit 7　　　　　　　　　　　　　　　　*43*
Possessive pronouns
Possessive form of nouns

Unit 8 — *50*
Simple past tense: affirmative, negative

Unit 9 — *58*
Simple past tense: interrogative

Unit 10 — *65*
Object pronouns

Unit 11 — *71*
Present progressive tense

Unit 12 — *77*
Simple present vs. present progressive
Frequency adverbs

Unit 13 — *83*
Can

Unit 14 — *90*
Future with *going to*

Unit 15 — *98*
Tense review

Introduction

English On Call is a three-level computer software/workbook series designed for student, young adult, and adult learners of English. Each of the fifteen units in the three levels consists of contextualized exercises that use humor, drama, general-interest topics, and even mystery to present and practice individual grammar points. In order to enhance students' awareness of natural spoken English, all the activities in the software and many exercises in the workbooks are presented in a continuous dialog format written in a casual conversational style. Learner control, active language manipulation, and the development of learning strategies have been emphasized in the design of the *English On Call* software.

Unit Organization and Content

Each unit is divided into three parts, as follows:

- *Workbook activities include recognition exercises that introduce the meaning and form of a structure, a grammar box that summarizes this information, and exercises that give students practice using the structure in meaningful contexts.*

- *Software activities include interactive presentations of the structure, contextualized grammar exercises, and text-reconstruction activities.*

- *More challenging follow-up workbook exercises give students the opportunity to see how the structure works in additional contexts. This section often includes open-ended, personalized activities.*

Although the software and workbook at each level are designed to be used together, both may also be used independently. A workbook unit provides sufficient coverage of each grammar point to stand on its own; and since the software units contain both a presentation and a grammar box along with the exercises, they can easily be plugged into any program as an independent supplement.

Classroom Uses

The software/workbook units may function in one or more of the following ways:

- *As individualized instruction for students who may be having problems with specific structures or concepts.*

- *As additional practice and reinforcement of structures in a contextualized and conversational format for full-class participation.*

- *As review and catch-up work for students who have already been exposed to the material at a different time and perhaps in a different learning environment.*

Series Organization and Content

An attempt has been made to control the use of vocabulary and secondary structures within the units so that they need not necessarily be presented in the sequence in which they appear in each level. Teachers and students should be able to pick and choose according to the needs of their curriculum. The structures included at each level are as follows:

Level One (beginning to low-intermediate)

Tenses and Modals
Simple Present–*to be*
Simple Present–all verbs
Simple Past
Present Progressive
Simple Present vs. Present Progressive
Can
Future with *going to*

Other Points
There is, There are
Subject Pronouns
WH-questions
Possessive Adjectives and Possessive Pronouns
Possessive Form of Nouns
Adverbs of Frequency
Object Pronouns

Level Two (intermediate)

Tenses and Modals
Will
Should and *Would*
Past Progressive
Might and *Must*
Present Perfect
Simple Past vs. Present Perfect
Present Perfect Progressive
Would and *Could*
Past Perfect

Other Points
Direct and Indirect Objects
Comparatives and Superlatives
Adverbial Clauses
Gerund vs. Infinitive

Level Three (high-intermediate to advanced)

Tenses and Modals
Reported Speech
Passive Voice
Past Modals
Real Conditional
Unreal Conditional–Present and Past
Causative Verbs–Active and Passive
Future Perfect

Other Points
Noun Clauses
Relative Clauses

UNIT 1

1 *Look at the parts of the computer.*

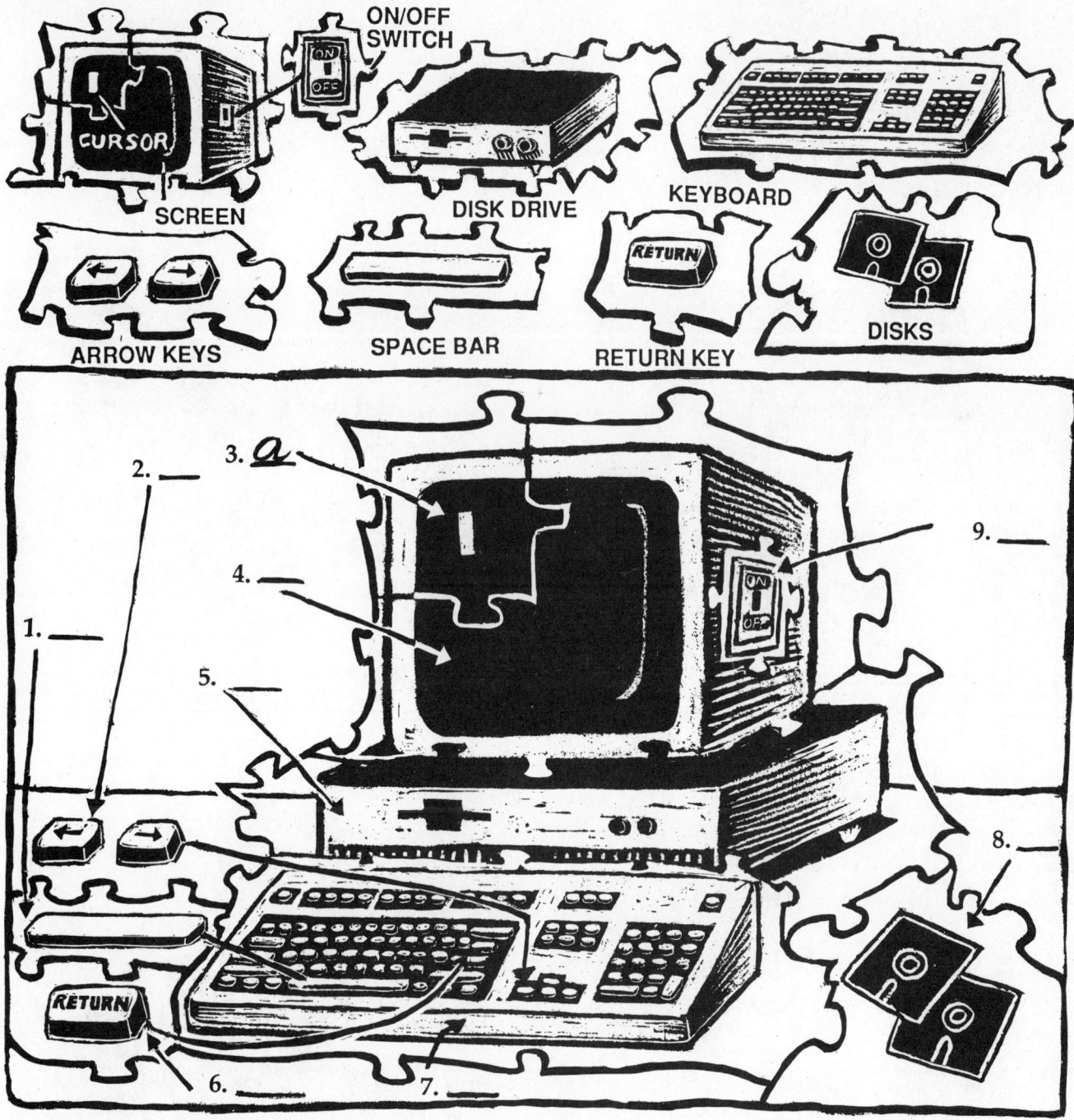

Now read the sentences and label the computer. Write the correct letter in each blank.

a. This is the cursor.
b. This is the screen.
c. These are the disks.
d. This is the off/on switch.
e. This is the disk drive.
f. These are the arrow keys.
g. This is the space bar.
h. This is the return key.
i. This is the keyboard.

2 Read the sentences. Then look at the pictures and write the correct sentences in the bubbles.

- They're the disks.
- It's a computer.
- No, it isn't. The light is off.
- Now it's on.

1.

2.

3.

4.

3 *Read the sentences. Then look at the pictures and write the correct sentences next to each picture. Some sentences can be used more than once.*

- Rick is at the computer.
- He's confused.
- The computer is on.
- The disk isn't in the disk drive.
- The disk is in the disk drive.
- Amy is at the computer.
- She isn't confused.
- Rick and Amy are at the computer.
- They aren't confused.

VOCABULARY BOX
confused

1. a. Amy is at the computer.
   b. The disk isn't in the disk drive.
   c. _____

2. a. _____
   b. _____
   c. _____

3. a. _____
   b. _____
   c. _____
   d. _____

GRAMMAR BOX

to be — Present Tense

Affirmative (+)	Contractions (')	Interrogative (?)	Negative (-)
I am	I'm	am I	I'm not
you are	you're	are you	you aren't
he is	he's	is he	he isn't
she is	she's	is she	she isn't
it is	it's	is it	it isn't
we are	we're	are we	we aren't
you are	you're	are you	you aren't
they are	they're	are they	they aren't
this is	—	is this	this isn't
these are	—	are these	these aren't

Note: You can also use these forms for the negative (-): you're not, he's not, she's not, it's not, we're not, they're not.

+		This is	a computer.	+	Two people are		at the computer.
?	Is	it	an IBM?	?	Are	they	teachers?
−	No,	it isn't.		−	No,	they aren't.	
+		It's	an Apple.	+		They're	college students.

4 Complete the story with 's (is), 're (are), or 'm (am).

Hello. I _____ Rick Daly, and this is
       1

my sister, Amy. She _____ 19 and
                        2

I _____ 15. We _____ both students.
   3   4

She _____ in her second year of college,
       5

and I _____ in high school.
         6

She _____ the computer expert
       7

in the family.

4

5 *Complete the conversation with the words in parentheses and the correct form of the verb* **to be.**

1. **A:** _Are you_ a student here?
   (you)

   B: No, _____ . _____ a teacher.
   (I, neg.)   (I)

2. **A:** What _____ ?
   (these)

   B: _____ disks for a computer.
   (they)

3. **A:** _____ here today.
   (George, neg.)

   B: Yes, _____ . _____ over there.
   (he)   (he)

   A: Oh, _____ right.
   (you)

4. **A:** _____ an arrow key?
   (this)

   B: No, _____ the return key. _____ the arrow keys.
   (it)   (these)

5. **A:** _____ here tonight?
   (your parents)

   B: No, _____ . _____ in Peru,
   (they, neg.)   (Dad)

   and _____ at work. _____ here alone.
   (Mom)   (we)

Now you're ready for the computer. When you finish at the computer, go to page 6.

6 *Amy is explaining the computer to Rick. Complete the conversation with* **this** *or* **these**.

AMY: OK, now. _These_₁ are the disks and _____₂ is the disk drive. There's a disk in the drive. _____₃ is the off/on switch. The lesson is on the screen. See?

RICK: Sure. It's easy.

AMY: Now, _____₄ is the return key and _____₅ are the arrow keys.

RICK: And what's _____₆ ?

AMY: That's the cursor.

7 *Look at this ad for the new BBM 411 computer. Then complete the ad with* **it** *or* **they** *and the correct form of the verb* **to be**. *Do not use contractions.*

COME IN TODAY AND SEE THE BBM 411 MINI!

This is the new BBM 411 mini computer. _It is_₁ small, _____₂ fast, and _____₃ cheap. These are the disks for the BBM 411 mini. _____₄ very small (_____₅ the size of a credit card!), but _____₆ very powerful and _____₇ cheap too.

Computer World
940 East Strand Road
Kansas City, Kansas

For more information, call (913) 882-5504.

8 Rick and Amy are at the high school the day before classes begin. They're talking to a new teacher. Complete the conversation with a pronoun and the correct form of the verb to be. Use contractions when you can and the negative when necessary.

```
PRONOUNS    BE
I           'm / am
you, we, they   're / are
he, she     's / is
```

RICK: <u>Are</u>₁ <u>you</u>₂ a new teacher?

MS. GRANT: Yes. <u>I'm</u>₃ the computer teacher.

RICK: Oh. ____₄ really interested in computers.

MS. GRANT: Good.

RICK: Amy is too. ____₅ the family computer expert.

MS. GRANT: ____₆ ____₇ a student here too, Amy?

AMY: No, ____₈ ____₉ in high school anymore. ____₁₀ in college now. ____₁₁ a sophomore. But Rick's still in school here. ____₁₂ a junior.

MS. GRANT: Are your parents here tonight?

AMY: No, ____₁₃ ____₁₄ . Mom is at work, and Dad is in Peru right now. ____₁₅ here alone.

MS. GRANT: Your Dad is in Peru?

RICK: Uh-huh. ____₁₆ a pilot.

MS. GRANT: Oh, I see.

7

UNIT 2

1 *Tourists are asking directions. Read the conversations. Then look at the maps on the next page (page 9) and write the correct conversation under each map. You will use only four of the conversations.*

a. A: Excuse me. Is there a coffee shop near here?

   B: No, there aren't any coffee shops around here, but there is a nice little restaurant in the park.

b. A: Are there any fast-food restaurants around here?

   B: There's a McDonalds across the street from the post office, and there's a Burger King under the subway bridge on Little Street.

c. A: Excuse me. Is there a bus stop near here?

   B: Sure. There's one in front of the Chinese restaurant on Second Street. It's under a big tree.

d. A: Excuse me. Is there a bank near here?

   B: Yes, there are two. There's one on the corner of Pine and Bradley, and there's one next to the post office on First Street.

e. A: Excuse me. Are there any good restaurants around here?

   B: Sorry. There aren't any restaurants near here, but there's a coffee shop over there.

f. A: Excuse me. Is there a bookstore around here?

   B: No, there isn't. But there's a newsstand on the first floor of the Bailey Building on Lincoln.

1. A: _____

   B: _____

2. A: _____

   B: _____

3. A: _____

   B: _____

4. A: _____

   B: _____

2 *Amy is talking to Mario, a student from Mexico. She's telling him about American weights and measures. Look at the chart. Then complete the conversation.*

WEIGHTS AND MEASUREMENTS

LINE MEASURE

	1 inch	=	2.54 centimeters (cm)	
12 inches (in)	=	1 foot		
3 feet (ft)	=	1 yard (yd)	=	0.9144 meters (m)
	1 mile (mi)	=	1.609 kilometers (km)	

WEIGHT

	1 ounce (oz)	=	28.35 grams (gm)
16 ounces	=	1 pound (lb)	=	0.4536 kilogram (kg)
	2.2 pounds	=	1 kilogram

CAPACITY (LIQUID) MEASURE

3 teaspoons (tsp)	=	1 tablespoon (tb)
16 tablespoons	=	1 cup (c)
2 cups	=	1 pint (pt)
2 pints	=	1 quart (qt) = 0.946 liter (l)
4 quarts	=	1 gallon (gal)

AMY: It's easy. There are __2.54__ centimeters in an inch, and _____ inches in a foot.
                  1   2

Then there are _____ feet in a yard, and there's a little more than _____ yard
                         3   4

in a meter.

MARIO: What about a mile?

AMY: Well, a mile is about _____ kilometers.
                                   5

MARIO: And weight? How much is a pound?

AMY: There are about _____ pounds in a kilogram. That's easy to remember.
                               6

Then there are the measures for liquid. We use cups. There are _____ cups,
                                                                        7

like a coffee cup, in a pint, and there are _____ pints in a quart.
                                                            8

There's a little more than _____ quart in a liter.
                                       9

GRAMMAR BOX

there is/there are

+	?	–
there is (there's)	is there	there isn't
there are	are there	there aren't

A: Excuse me. Is there a bank around here?
B: No, there isn't, but there's a cash machine on the corner.
A: Are there any good Italian restaurants near here?
B: Well, there are two good restaurants —French and Chinese— but there aren't any Italian restaurants.

3 Complete the conversation with there's, there are, Is there, or Are there.

AMY: _____ anything good on TV tonight?
                     1

RICK: Well, _____ a news program at 7:00 and then _____ some
                        2   3
old cartoons from 8:00 to 9:00.

AMY: Is that all?

RICK: _____ a special program about snakes at 8:00.
              4

AMY: Ugh. _____ any movies on?
                    5

RICK: Yeah. _____ one at 11:00—*Jaws*—and then _____
                      6   7
two old movies at 12:00—*It Happened One Night* and *Casablanca*.

AMY: That's too late. _____ a ball game on?
                                8

RICK: No. Not tonight.

AMY: That's too bad. How boring!

4 Complete the article from the Barker News with is, are, isn't, or aren't.

TRAVEL WORLD
Inexpensive Hotels in the Region—The Biltmore

George Merlo

The Biltmore is a wonderful hotel. It has almost everything. The rooms are big and comfortable, and there _____(1) a color TV in all of them. There _____(2) also two double beds in every room and a small table with chairs. One problem is that there _____(3) (neg.) any pictures on the wall and there _____(4) (neg.) a big mirror. Every hotel room needs at least one picture and a big mirror!

For people who like exercise, there _____(5) a beautiful pool on the top floor and there _____(6) a health club in the basement. In the club there _____(7) bicycles and weights, and there _____(8) also a sauna! All of this is free.

There _____(9) two nice restaurants in the hotel and there _____(10) a coffee shop on the first floor. Another problem is that there _____(11) (neg.) a newsstand in the hotel and there _____(12) (neg.) any shops. But there _____(13) a big drugstore and a newsstand near the hotel, so it is only a small problem. All in all, this hotel is excellent.

Now you're ready for the computer.
When you finish at the computer, go to page 13.

5 *Look at the maps. Then complete the conversation under each map. Use the words in parentheses in your conversations.*

1. **A:** Excuse me. _____ _____ _____ bank near here?

   B: (next to) _____
   _____
   _____

2. **A:** _____ _____ any coffee shops around here?

   B: (on) _____
   _____

3. **A:** _____ _____ _____ park near here?

   B: (on, between) _____
   _____
   _____

4. **A:** Excuse me. _____ _____ any fast-food places around here?

   B: (in, across from) _____
   _____
   _____

6 *Mario is telling María about his room at home. Read the first part of the description. Then complete the description.*

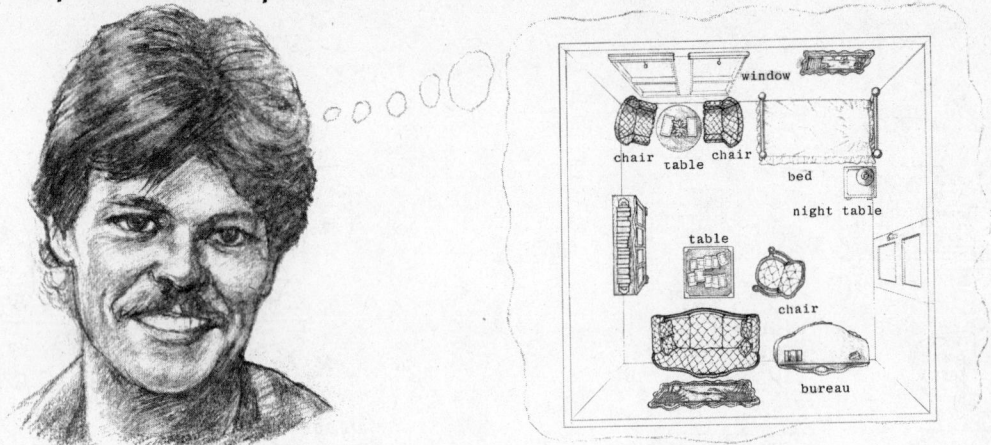

Well, my room is big —about 15 feet by 15 feet. There are two big windows. In front of the windows there are two big chairs and a small round table. In one corner there is a big bureau and in the other corner there is a small bed. Next to the bed _____

_____

_____

7 *Now draw a picture of your bedroom. Then write a description.*

UNIT 3

1 Rick is taking a test in his geography class. Look at the map of Australia. Then read Rick's answers (A) and choose the correct questions.

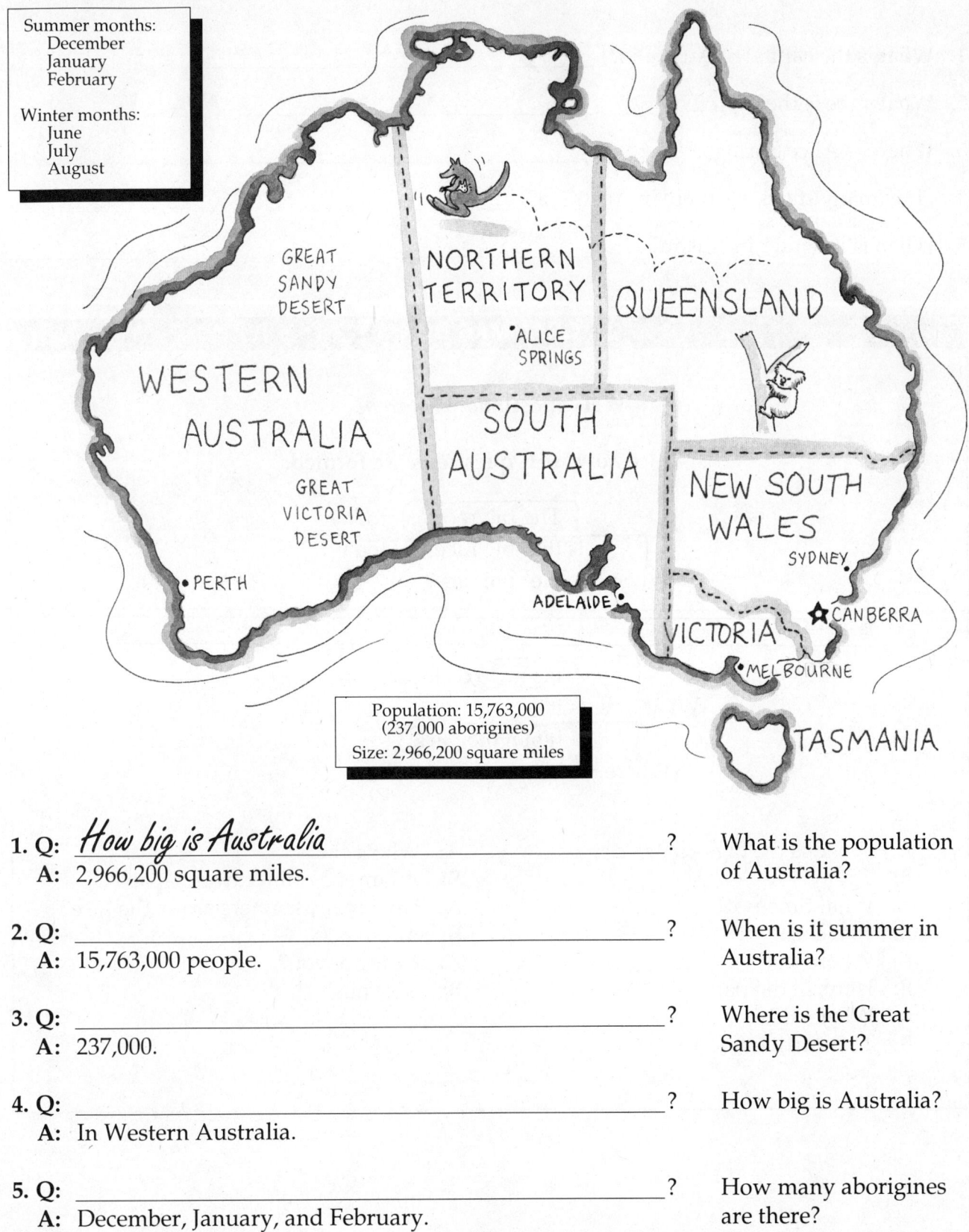

1. **Q:** *How big is Australia*_____?   What is the population
   A: 2,966,200 square miles.   of Australia?

2. **Q:** _____?   When is it summer in
   A: 15,763,000 people.   Australia?

3. **Q:** _____?   Where is the Great
   A: 237,000.   Sandy Desert?

4. **Q:** _____?   How big is Australia?
   A: In Western Australia.

5. **Q:** _____?   How many aborigines
   A: December, January, and February.   are there?

2 Look again at the map of Australia on page 15 and answer these questions.

1. What is the capital of Australia? _____
2. What state is the capital in? _____
3. Where is Alice Springs? _____
4. How many states are there in Australia? _____
5. When is it winter in Australia? _____

GRAMMAR BOX

WH- questions with *to be*

Notice how WH- questions are formed:

The big race (is) today.
Is the big race (today?)
When is the big race?

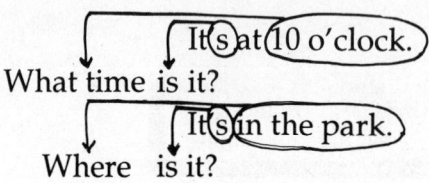
What time is it?
Where is it?

A: When is the big race?   A: Who's she?
B: Today!   B: A famous runner from Japan.
A: What time is it?   A: How many runners are in the race?
B: 10 o'clock.   B: About 400.
A: Where is it?   A: How are you?
B: Here, in the park.   B: Nervous!
A: What's this?
B: The starting line.

3 *Rick is talking to a new student. Complete the conversation with* **who, where, what time, is,** *or* **are.**

HELEN: Excuse me. ___Where___ 's the biology room?

RICK: Over there. In Room 211.

HELEN: Thanks. _____ 's the biology teacher?

RICK: Ms. Rogers.

HELEN: _____ she good?

RICK: She's OK. _____ you new here?

HELEN: Yes. I'm Helen Chung.

RICK: Nice to meet you, Helen. I'm Rick Daly. _____ are you from?

HELEN: I'm from Korea.

RICK: Really?

HELEN: Uh-huh. _____ is it?

RICK: It's 10:10.

HELEN: Oh dear. It's time for class. See you later.

RICK: Bye.

4 *Look at the pictures and complete the questions. Use contractions in your questions when you can. Then answer the questions. You don't have to use complete sentences in your answers.*

QUESTION WORDS	BE
Who }	's
What }	
Where }	are
How }	
What time	is
How many (+ noun)	are

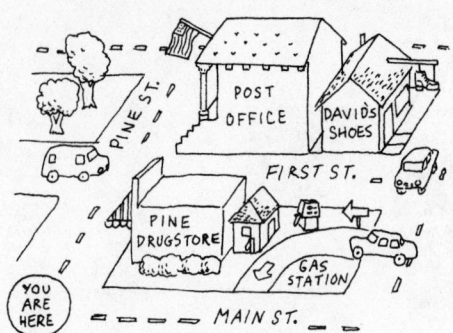

1. A: Excuse me. __Where's__ the post office?

   B: __On Pine Street.__

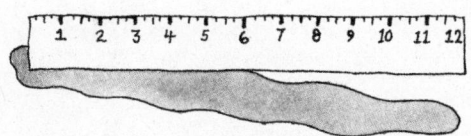

2. A: _____ inches _____ there in a foot?

   B: _____

3. A: _____ those people?

   B: _____

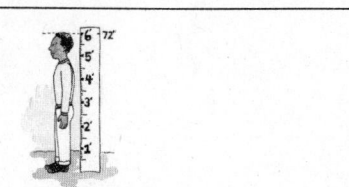

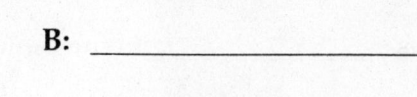

4. A: _____ tall _____ Jeff?

   B: _____

5. A: _____ it?

   B: _____

6. A: _____ in the car with Rick?

   B: _____

7. A: _____ in that box?

   B: _____

Now you're ready for the computer. When you finish at the computer, go to page 19.

5 Look at the map of Canada and write questions with the words in parentheses. Then answer the questions.

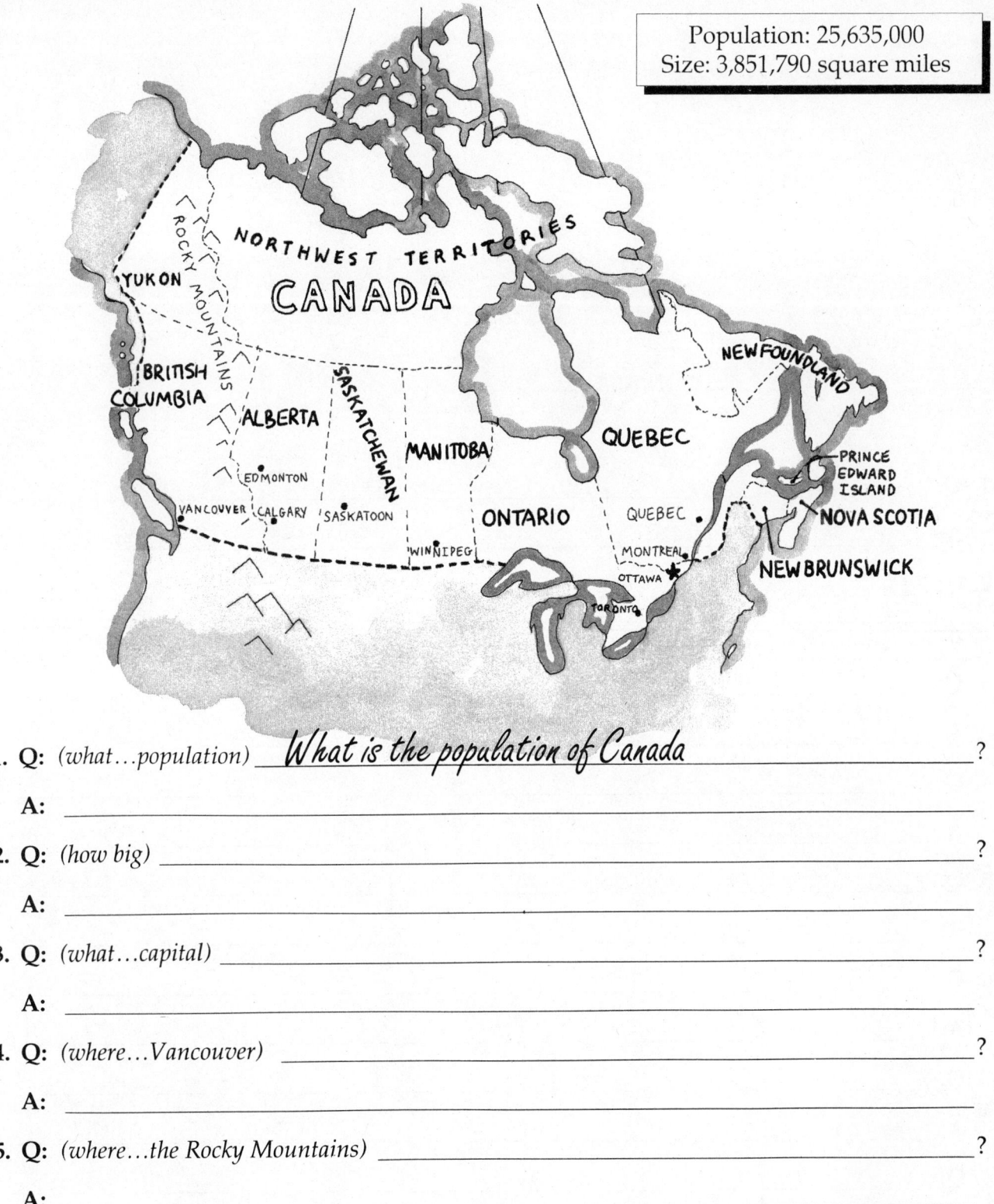

Population: 25,635,000
Size: 3,851,790 square miles

1. Q: (what...population) *What is the population of Canada* ?
   A: _____
2. Q: (how big) _____ ?
   A: _____
3. Q: (what...capital) _____ ?
   A: _____
4. Q: (where...Vancouver) _____ ?
   A: _____
5. Q: (where...the Rocky Mountains) _____ ?
   A: _____

6 *Draw a map of the country you live in. Then write eight questions about the country. If possible, exchange workbooks with a friend or classmate and see if he or she can answer the questions. You can look at the questions on page 19 if you need help.*

1. Q: _____?
   A: _____
2. Q: _____?
   A: _____
3. Q: _____?
   A: _____
4. Q: _____?
   A: _____
5. Q: _____?
   A: _____
6. Q: _____?
   A: _____
7. Q: _____?
   A: _____
8. Q: _____?
   A: _____

UNIT 4

1 *Read the sentences. Then look at the pictures from news stories in the **Barker News** and write the correct sentence under each picture.*

Rafael García is receiving his check. "Mr. García, here is your check for $5,000,000."

Ralph Cory, 18, is usually on his bicycle by 5:00 in the morning.

"I'm 82 years old, my mother is 102, and my father is 103."

At this zoo, the animals are almost never in their cages. This tiger and its cubs are free.

The water is very high, but Mary and Bill Kelly are still in their house beside the Cory River. "This is our home," they said, "and we won't leave."

The President is talking to a group of parents at the White House. "Your children are our future," he said.

1. _____

2. _____

3. _____

4. _____

5. _____

6. _____

GRAMMAR BOX

Possessive Adjectives

I → my
you → your
he → his
she → her
it → its

we → our
you → your
they → their

A: Mary, is this your car?
B: No, my car is over there. Maybe it belongs to the Thomsons. Their car is red.
A: No, they're not here today. Tom is here, isn't he? Maybe that's his car.
B: Yes, you're right! His books are on the back seat.

2 *Complete the conversations with* **my, her, his, their, your, its,** *or* **our.**

1. WHAT'S THAT IN BILL'S CAR? OH, THAT'S _____ PET SNAKE.

2. AND THIS IS WHERE PETE AND I LIVE. THAT'S _____ LITTLE DOG, MILDRED. MY PARENTS LIVE NEXT DOOR. THAT'S _____ CAT, BOZO.

3. WHO'S THAT WITH ELIZABETH? OH, THAT'S _____ FATHER.

4. EXCUSE ME. IS THIS _____ EARRING? YES. THANKS VERY MUCH.

5. EXCUSE ME, BUT I THINK THAT'S _____ SUITCASE. OH. UH... SORRY.

6. NO, NOT THAT ONE. _____ LEAVES ARE ALL YELLOW.

22

3 *Mario is showing Amy pictures of his family in Mexico. Complete the conversation with* my, her, his, their, your, *or* our.

MARIO: This is ___my___ sister, Lupe,
with _____ two daughters, Ana and María.
                2

AMY: And who's this?

MARIO: Oh, that's _____ brother, Marcos,
                            3
and _____ wife, Silvia. And that's _____
       4   5
house behind them.

AMY: Are these _____ parents?
                        6
MARIO: Yes. And that's _____ house.
                                   7

Fill in the blanks. Then write who it is.

1. ___Her___ daughters are Ana and María. ___Lupe___
2. _____ house is very old. _____
3. _____ husband is Marcos. _____

Now write more sentences like these and ask someone you know to fill in the blanks and say who it is. You can write about any of the people in this unit or about the people in your class.

1. ___His car is blue. (the teacher)___
2. _____
3. _____
4. _____

Now you're ready for the computer. When you finish at the computer, go to page 24.

23

4 *Ann Daly is showing Amy, Rick, and Mario an old picture of her family. Complete the conversation.*

ANN: These are my great-grandparents, and that's _____ wagon. And those are _____ three children.

Now write Ann's sentences again. Change **great-grandparents** *to* **great-grandmother** *and make all the other necessary changes.*

ANN: _____

_____

_____

Now change **great-grandparents** *to* **great-grandfather** *and make all the other necessary changes.*

ANN: _____

_____

_____

5 Complete the conversation with possessive adjectives.

ANN: Oh, no! I'm late. Where's _____ umbrella?

BOB: Isn't it in the closet?

ANN: No. Oh, well, here's _____ raincoat. I can use that. Bye.

*Now write Ann and Bob's conversation again. Change **I** to **you** and make all the other necessary changes.*

ANN: _____

BOB: _____

ANN: _____

6 Complete the conversation with the correct possessive adjective.

AMY: What's wrong with Mary? Why is she crying?

RICK: I think _____ leg is broken.

*Now write Amy and Rick's conversation again. Change **Mary** to **Joe's dog** and make all the other necessary changes.*

AMY: _____

RICK: _____

7 Complete the postcard with possessive adjectives.

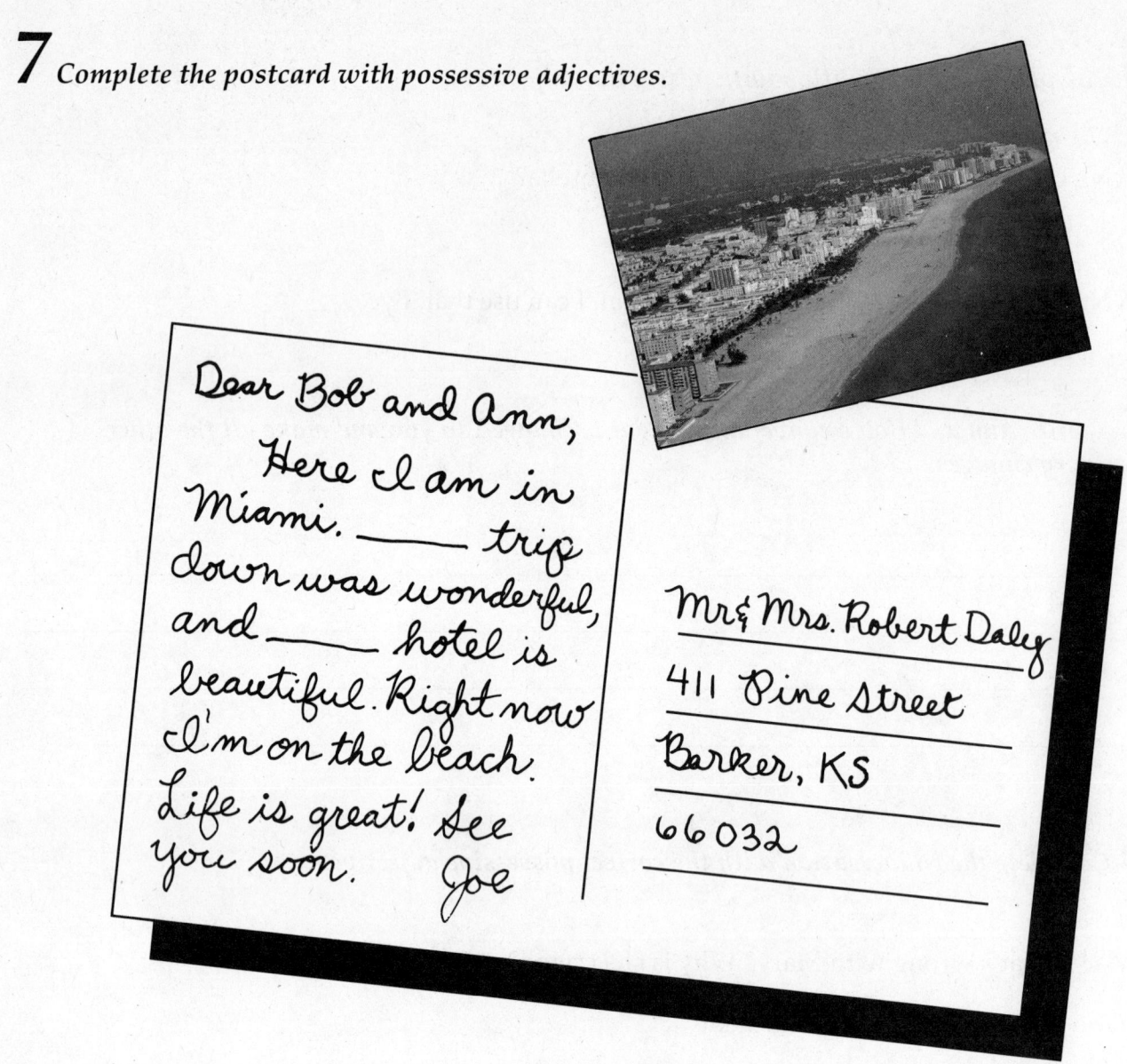

Dear Bob and Ann,
 Here I am in Miami. ____ trip down was wonderful, and ____ hotel is beautiful. Right now I'm on the beach. Life is great! See you soon.
    Joe

Mr & Mrs. Robert Daley
411 Pine Street
Barker, KS
66032

Now write Joe's postcard again. Change **I** to **Joan and I** and make all the necessary changes.

_____,

_____
_____
_____

UNIT 5

1 *Read the sentences. Then look at the treasure map. Choose the sentences that tell how to find the treasure and write them under the map.*

- Cross the river.
- Go into the small house.
- Go to the top of the hill.
- Walk down the hill toward the little river.
- Dig here.
- Walk to the small palm tree.
- Go to the turtle rock.
- Climb up the tree.
- Stand at the head of the turtle and take ten steps west.
- Stand at the head of the turtle and take eleven steps.

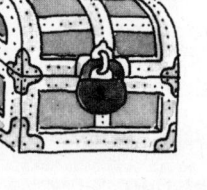

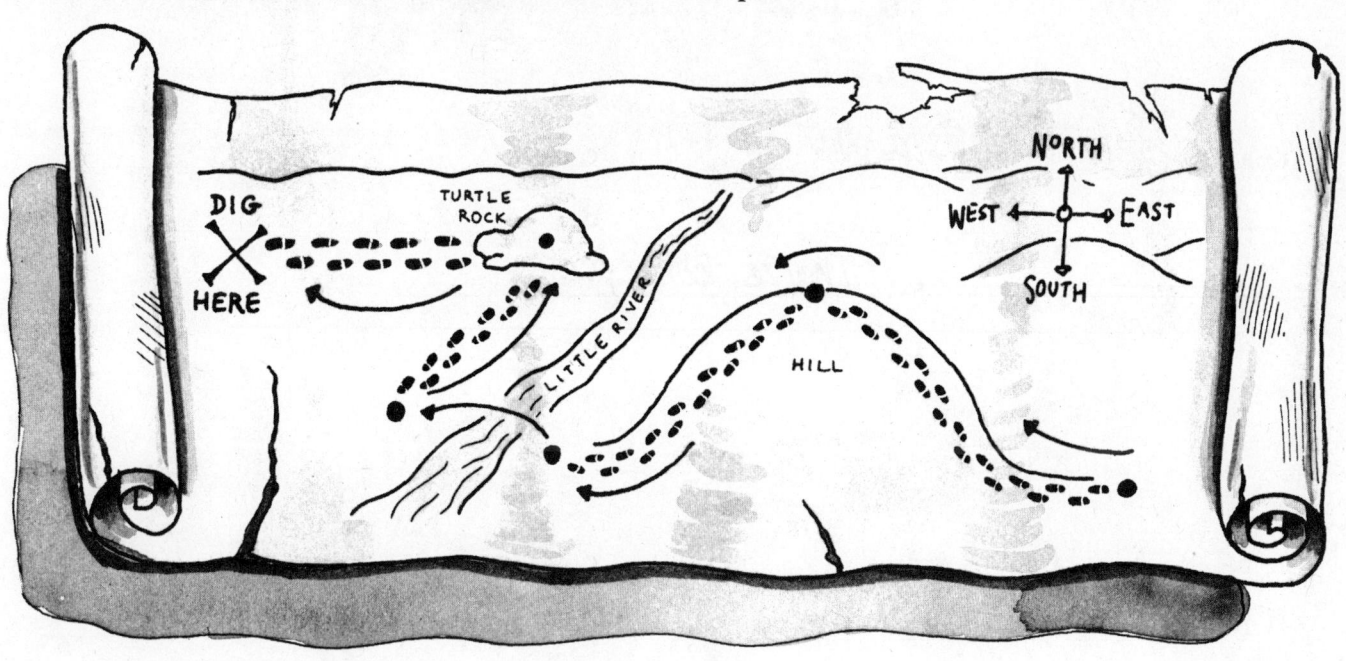

a. _____
b. _____
c. _____
d. _____
e. _____
f. _____

2 *Read the sentences. Then look at the pictures and write the correct sentences under each picture.*

- They're both pretty.
- Mike has a T-shirt on.
- It has two doors.
- Don has straight hair.
- They both have blond hair.
- Jennifer has a hat on.
- They both have four wheels.
- Maryann has long hair.

- They both wear glasses.
- It has four doors.
- Don has a tie on.
- Jennifer has short curly hair.
- Mike has curly hair.
- Maryann wears glasses.
- They both have dark hair and dark eyes.

1. a. _Jennifer has a hat on._   c. _____
   b. _____   d. _____
   e. _They're both pretty._
   f. _____

2. a. _____   c. _____
   b. _____   d. _____
   e. _____
   f. _____

3. a. _____   b. _____
   c. _____

3 Complete these sentences about yourself.

1. I have _____ eyes.
   (color)
2. I have _____ hair.
   (color)
3. I have _____ _____ hair.
   (long/short)   (curly/straight)

Now write about you and a family member or friend who looks like you.

_____ and I have _____ eyes. We both have _____ hair.
                                                              (color)

We both have _____ _____ hair too.
              (long/short) (curly/straight)

4 Pretend that you are the silhouette in each of the pictures. You are talking to the other person in the picture. Read the sentences. Then look at the pictures and write the correct sentences next to each picture.

- I have a pencil.
- We both have a magazine.
- You have a radio.

- I have a camera.
- We both have bicycles.
- You have some flowers.

1. a. _____
   b. _____
   c. _____

2. a. _____
   b. _____
   c. _____

5 These questions are about you. Cross out the wrong answer.

1. Do you live with your family?   a) Yes, I do.   b) No, I don't.

2. Do you live in an apartment?   a) Yes, I do.   b) No, I don't.

3. Do you and your family see each other often?   a) Yes, we do.   b) No, we don't.

4. Does your father work for an airline?   a) Yes, he does.   b) No, he doesn't.

5. Does your mother have her own business?   a) Yes, she does.   b) No, she doesn't.

6. Do your best friends live near you?   a) Yes, they do.   b) No, they don't.

GRAMMAR BOX

Simple Present

Affirmative (+)	Interrogative (?)	Negative (-)	Short answers (+)	(-)
I play	do I play	I don't play	Yes, I do.	No, I don't.
you play	do you play	you don't play	Yes, you do.	No, you don't.
he plays	does he play	he doesn't play	Yes, he does.	No, he doesn't.
she plays	does she play	she doesn't play	Yes, she does.	No, she doesn't.
it plays	does it play	it doesn't play	Yes, it does.	No, it doesn't.
we play	do we play	we don't play	Yes, we do.	No, we don't.
you play	do you play	you don't play	Yes, you do.	No, you don't.
they play	do they play	they don't play	Yes, they do.	No, they don't.

Imperative: Play!

NOTE: Verbs ending in *s, z, sh, ch, x,* or *o* add *-es* for the he/she/it form: I teach, he teaches; you go, she goes; we wash, it washes.

A: I love baseball! Look at Tom! He really plays well.
B: I know. Sometimes he hits the ball out of the field.
A: Do you like football too?
B: No, I don't. It's too violent. But I really like soccer.
A: Oh, I do too. I have tickets for the next game. Do you want to go?
B: Yes, great!

6 *Complete the conversations by filling in the boxes with* **do** *or* **does** *and the blanks with the correct form of the verb in parentheses.*

1. Rick and his friend Joe are talking about sports.

    JOE: [Does] your father _like_ baseball?
    (like)

    RICK: No. But he _____ football and basketball.
    (like)

    JOE: What about you?

    RICK: I _____ baseball.
    (like)

    JOE: [   ] you _____ baseball?
    (play)

    RICK: Sometimes. But I _____ soccer every Saturday.
    (play)

2. Ann and her friend Sylvia are talking about telephones.

    SYLVIA: [   ] your children _____ their own phone?
    (have)

    ANN: No, we _____ just one phone.
    (have)

    SYLVIA: We _____ three!
    (have)

    ANN: Three? Really?

    SYLVIA: Well, my kids _____ teenagers. My husband and I _____ one phone,
    (be) (have)
    my son _____ one, and my daughter _____ one.
    (have) (have)

    ANN: [   ] your son _____ on the phone a lot?
    (talk)

    SYLVIA: Yes, he _____ more than my daughter.
    (talk)

    ANN: [   ] they _____ for their phones or [   ] you _____ ?
    (pay) (pay)

    SYLVIA: They both _____ after school, so they _____ part of the bill every month.
    (work) (pay)
    My daughter _____ at Burger King, and my son _____ cars at the car
    (work) (wash)
    wash on Spruce Street.

31

7 *Look at the pictures and complete the questions with* **do** *or* **does**. *Then answer the questions with short answers.*

Steffi Graf

Paul Newman

Fly

Whale

New York Yankees

1. __Do__ whales breathe air? __Yes, they do.__
2. _____ a fly have eight legs? _____
3. _____ Paul Newman like racing? _____
4. _____ New York have a baseball team? _____
5. _____ Steffi Graf work in a bank? _____
6. _____ your parents live near you? _____
7. _____ you work? _____
8. _____ you and your family have pets? _____

8 *Pretend that the man in the picture is talking to you. Complete his questions with* **do** *or* **does**. *Then answer the questions with short answers.*

1. _____ I have my glasses? _____
2. _____ you have my English book? _____
3. _____ I have my keys? _____

Now you're ready for the computer. When you finish at the computer, go to page 33.

9 *Look at the treasure map. Then complete the instructions under the map.*

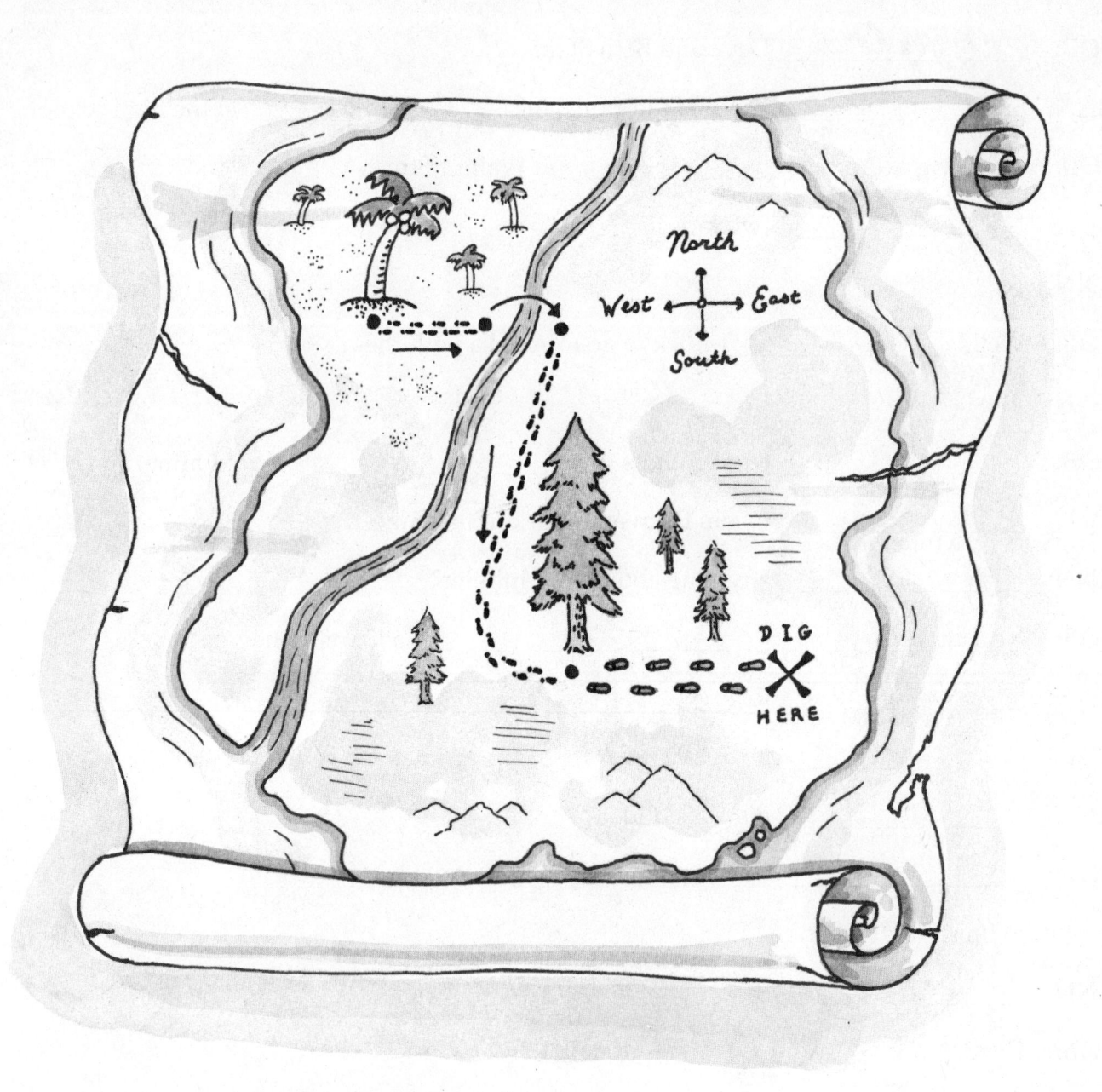

<u>*Start*</u> at the big palm tree. _____ east to the river. _____ the
   1   2   3
river. _____ south to the big pine tree. _____ eight steps east from the
         4   5
tree. _____ here.
         6

10 *Complete the conversation with the words in parentheses. Be sure to use the correct form of the verb.*

BOB: <u>Do you know</u> Dave and Beth Stanley?
(1. you/know)

ANN: Sure. _____ at the bank, and _____ at the high school.
(2. he/work) (3. she/teach)

BOB: That's right. And _____ on Walnut Street.
(4. they/live)
_____ two kids.
(5. they/have)

ANN: So?

BOB: Well, _____ Rick to go to Alaska with them.
(6. they/want)

ANN: Alaska? Why?

BOB: _____ two brothers there. _____ a gold mine, and
(7. Dave/have) (8. they/have)
_____ to join them and work in the mine.
(9. Dave/want)

ANN: _____ anything about gold mining?
(10. Dave/know)

BOB: No, but _____ _____ a lot of money.
(11. he/say) (12. his brothers/make)

ANN: _____ to go?
(13. Rick/want)

BOB: _____ he does.
(14. he/say)

ANN: _____ it's a good idea?
(15. you/think)

BOB: _____ _____ crazy. _____
(16. I/think) (17. it/be) (18. he/have)
to finish high school.

ANN: _____ .
(19. I/agree)

BOB: Good. Now _____ to talk to Rick.
(20. we/have)

11 *Pretend that it's the first day of class. You have to introduce yourself to your classmates. Read the examples. Then write out what you are going to say.*

My name is Amy Daly. I'm a student, and I live in an apartment on Maple Avenue. I'm from Barker, Kansas. My family lives in a small house there. My father works for Skyway Airlines, and my mother is a reporter. My brother goes to Barker High School. I study a lot. But in my free time, I swim and play with my computer. On weekends, my friends and I have parties, or we go to the movies. Sometimes we go to football or basketball games.

My name is Bob Daly. I'm a pilot, and I work for Skyway Airlines. I'm married, and I have two children. My wife is a reporter, and my children are both students. I work hard. But in my free time, I read, go to the movies, and watch football games on TV. On weekends, my family and I clean the house and go shopping. Sometimes we invite friends over for dinner. In the summer, I like to play tennis. In the winter, I ski.

UNIT 6

1 *Read the sentences. Then look at the pictures and write the correct sentence or sentences under each picture.*

- She is from India.
- She looks Latin American.
- It doesn't have bones.
- They go to school in Peru.
- They don't go to school in a city.
- They don't eat meat.
- It doesn't see color.
- They have four stomachs.

VOCABULARY BOX

bones   meat

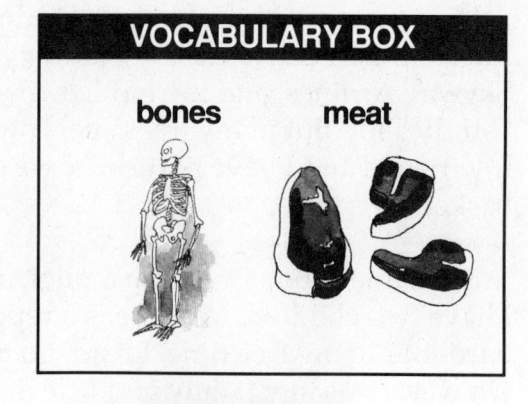

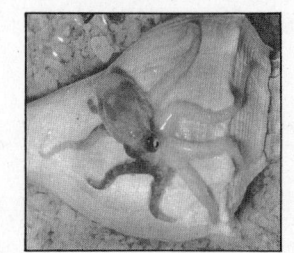

1. a. _____

2. a. _____

3. a. _____
   b. _____

4. a. _____

5. a. _____

6. a. _____
   b. _____

2 *Look at the pictures. Then read the questions and choose the correct answers.*

1. What do Bob and Ann Daly do?
   _____

2. Where does Ann work?
   _____

3. When does she work?
   _____

4. How do they get to work?
   _____

5. How often does Bob fly?
   _____

Four times a week.

At the *Barker News*.

Ann drives, and Bob takes the bus.

He's a pilot, and she's a reporter.

She works from 4:00 to 11:00 five days a week.

Now answer these questions on your own. You don't have to use complete sentences.

1. Where do the Dalys live?
   _____

2. Who cleans the bathroom in the Daly family?
   _____

3. Who washes the dishes?
   _____

3 *Choose a word or expression from each of the columns and write sentences about you and your family.*

I		cats.
My father		to swim.
My mother		to fly.
My sister	like/likes	to watch TV.
My brother	don't like/doesn't like	to go dancing.
My brothers and sisters		pizza.
My grandparents		coffee.

1. *My sister doesn't like to fly.*
2. _____
3. _____
4. _____
5. _____
6. _____
7. _____
8. _____

GRAMMAR BOX

WH- questions, negatives —Simple Present

Notice how the negative is formed:

    She　　likes movies.　　　　They　　like　movies.
    She doesn't like sad movies.　　They don't　like　comedies.

Notice how WH- questions are formed:

    She likes movies.
    Does she like movies?
    What does she like?

A: I love to go to the movies, but I don't like sad movies.
B: There's a comedy tonight at the Roxy Theater.
A: What time does it start?
B: The first show is at 7:00.
A: That's too early. My class doesn't end until 7:30.

4 Look at this ad for the new DR12 robot. Then use the words in the box to write a sentence under each picture.

| complain | take messages | wash the dishes | clean the house |
| talk | make the beds | eat | sleep |

THE PERFECT FRIEND
– DR12 –
It Makes Your World Happy!

1. *It talks.*
2. _____
3. _____  
4. _____
5. _____  
6. _____
7. _____  
8. _____

Get yours today. Call (800) 602-9035

5 *Ann Daly is interviewing the robot for the* **Barker News.** *Complete the conversation with* do, does, don't, doesn't, is, 's, 're, *or* are.

ANN: How many DR12 robots _____ there?
         1

DR12: Oh, only about 100, I think. And we _____ all different, you know.
         2

ANN: That _____ interesting. How _____ you different?
        3   4

DR12: Well, we all have different personalities, and we all look a little different. See, my monitor is yellow.

ANN: Yes, I see. Where _____ you get your energy, DR12?
                     5

DR12: From a big battery.

ANN: Where _____ your battery?
              6

DR12: Inside my head. Here.

ANN: How long _____ a battery last? A year?
                 7

DR12: Oh, no. It _____ last that long. It lasts exactly two months.
                    8

ANN: That _____ not very long.
             9

DR12: I know.

ANN: What _____ you do at night?
             10

DR12: Oh, I work. But I do quiet work. I _____ want to wake people up.
                                            11

ANN: Finally, DR12, just what _____ DR12 mean?
                                 12

DR12: Oh, gosh. I _____ know! But I'll ask my maker and tell you tomorrow.
                     13

ANN: OK. Thanks.

Now you're ready for the computer. When you finish at the computer, go to page 41.

6 Ann's father, Bill Leak, is talking to a travel agent. He wants to go from New York to Miami. Write questions with the words in parentheses.

AGENT: *What day do you want to leave?*
(1. what day/you/want to leave)

BILL: On Thursday, January 15th.

AGENT: OK. What time do you want to leave?
(2. what time/you/want to leave)

BILL: Are there any planes in the morning?
(3. any planes/in the morning)

AGENT: There are three planes in the morning: one at 8:00, one at 10:00, and one at 11:30.

BILL: The 11:30 flight is good.

AGENT: But that one makes a stop.

BILL: Where does it stop?
(4. where/it/stop)

AGENT: In Atlanta.

BILL: That's OK. Do we get lunch?
(5. we/get/lunch)

AGENT: No, you don't get lunch, but you get a snack.

BILL: Which airport does it leave from?
(6. which airport/it/leave from)

AGENT: It leaves from Kennedy. Oh, when do you plan to return?
(7. when/you/plan to return)

BILL: On February 1st, in the afternoon.

AGENT: OK. There's a flight at 1:30. It gets into Kennedy at 5:30.

BILL: Does it make any stops?
(8. it/make any stops)

AGENT: Yes. It stops in Atlanta.

BILL: Do they serve dinner?
(9. they/serve/dinner)

AGENT: No, just a snack.

BILL: That sounds fine. Please send the tickets to my office.

7 *Pretend that you're talking to a man or woman you like a lot. Tell the person what you think of him or her. Read the examples. Then write out what you're going to say.*

You have beautiful eyes.
You look wonderful today.
You don't understand me.
You don't love me.

_____
_____
_____
_____

8 *Write four sentences describing a good teacher.*

1. *A good teacher listens to students.*
2. *A good teacher doesn't make fun of students.*
3. _____
4. _____
5. _____
6. _____

Now write four sentences describing a good student.

1. _____
2. _____
3. _____
4. _____

UNIT 7

1 *Where do you think these people live? Look at the pictures. Then read the phrases in the box. Write the correct phrase next to each house.*

MAP OF MOVIE STARS' HOUSES

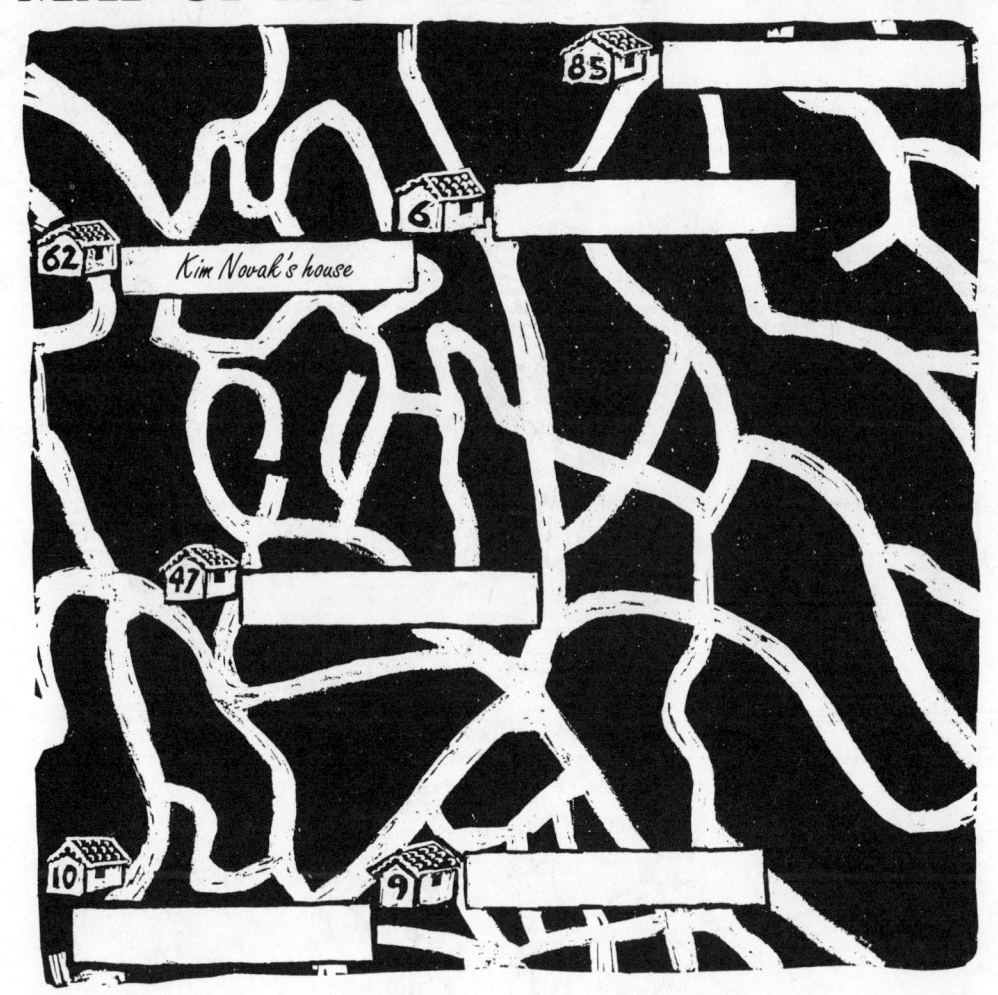

Kim Novak's house

The Bronsons (10)

Marlo Thomas (85)

Kim Novak (62)

Lloyd Bridges (9)

Debbie Boone (6)

Tom Jones (47)

Debbie Boone's house
Tom Jones's house
The Bronsons' house
Kim Novak's house
Lloyd Bridges's house
Marlo Thomas's house

2 *Pets often look like their owners. Who do these animals belong to? Complete the sentences.*

1. "My dog is a bulldog."

   a dachshund
   a poodle
   an Irish setter

   Theirs is _____.

   His is _____. Hers is _____.

2. "My cat is a Rex."

   a Persian
   a Siamese
   a Russian Blue

   His is _____.

   Hers is _____. Theirs is _____.

3 *Whose dogs are these? Look at the picture and complete the sentences.*

Speech bubbles:
- My dog is a _____1_____.
- Mine is a _____2_____.
- Ours is a _____3_____.
- Ours is a _____4_____.
- Mine is a collie.

Labels: greyhound, German shepherd, St. Bernard, pug, collie

GRAMMAR BOX

Possessive Pronouns and Nouns

I	→	my	→	mine
you	→	your	→	yours
he	→	his	→	his
she	→	her	→	hers
it	→	its	→	
we	→	our	→	ours
you	→	your	→	yours
they	→	their	→	theirs

Note the following possessive forms of nouns:

Mary	→	Mary's	John Brown	→	John Brown's
Thomas	→	Thomas's	the Browns	→	the Browns'
the dog	→	the dog's	the dogs	→	the dogs'

A: Are these your keys?
B: No, mine are upstairs. Terry has hers with her, and the children always take theirs to school.
A: Then they must be Ben's.
B: Oh, that's right. They're probably his.

45

4 Look at the pictures. Then complete the sentences and write the correct sentences under each picture. Some sentences can be used more than once.

- _____ is an IBM PC.
- _____ is a Compaq.
- _____ is a Panasonic.
- _____ is a Macintosh.
- _____ has one disk drive.

- _____ has two disk drives.
- _____ has a green monitor.
- _____ has an amber monitor.
- _____ has a black and white monitor.
- _____ has a color monitor.

1. a. *Mine is an IBM PC.*
   b. _____
   c. _____

2. a. *His is a Compaq.*
   b. _____
   c. _____

3. a. _____
   b. _____
   c. _____

4. a. _____
   b. _____
   c. _____

46

5 Complete the signs with 's or '.

1. Ruth's Café
2. THE WALTERS' FISH HOUSE
3. Bess's Flowers
4. The Harrises' BAR AND GRILL
5. MICHAEL'S BAR
6. HANK AND DICK'S PLACE

6 Complete the conversations with **mine, yours, ours, his, hers,** or **theirs**.

1. Is that your car?
   No. _____ Mine _____ is over there.

2. Please get me the file for Dick Borger and the one for Mr. and Mrs. Silver.
   I have Mr. Borger's right here, but I don't have _____ theirs _____.

3. Are these papers _____ mine _____?
   Oh, yes, they are. Thanks.

4. That's my sister's painting.
   But there are three. Which one is _____ hers _____?

5. Are these your keys, or are they Dave's?
   They aren't _____ mine _____ or _____ his _____. I think they're Frank and Jean's.

Now you're ready for the computer. When you finish at the computer, go to page 48.

7 *Read the article from the Barker News. The underlined words are not correct. Write the article again and correct the mistakes.*

SEE SPOT RUN

Mr. and Mrs. Pendalton of Atlanta, Georgia are furious at their neighbors, the Hesses. The <u>Pendaltons</u>¹ dog, Filly, a beautiful Irish setter, just had eight puppies. The problem is, all of <u>Fillys</u>² puppies look just like the <u>neighbors</u>³ dog, Jess. Jess is a very nice dog, but <u>Jess</u>⁴ family line is not as cute as <u>Fillys</u>⁵. In other words, Jess is a mutt.

The Pendaltons say that it is the <u>Hesses</u>⁶ responsibility to take care of <u>Fillys</u>⁷ puppies. The Hesses say it is the <u>Pendaltons</u>⁸. "How do we know that these are our <u>dogs</u>⁹ puppies?" said Mr. Hess. "Of course, the puppies are <u>Jess</u>¹⁰," said Mrs. Pendalton. "Poor Filly. She's such a good girl, and the <u>Hesses</u>¹¹ dog is so horrible."

Mr. and Mrs. Pendalton of Atlanta,

8 *Mario is showing Ann pictures of his family. Complete the conversation with a possessive adjective, a possessive pronoun, or 's or '.*

ANN: Is this _your_ house?

MARIO: No. _Ours_ has a wall around it. That one is my brother _____₃.
You see, _____₄ doesn't have a wall, and it has only two stories. _____₅ has three.

ANN: Are those _____₆ sister _____₇ children?

MARIO: No. _____₈ are a lot younger. Those are the neighbors _____₉ children.

ANN: What about these cute dogs? Is one of them _____₁₀?

MARIO: Yes, the black and white one is _____₁₁. _____₁₂ name is Lily. The other two are the neighbor _____₁₃.

ANN: And is that _____₁₄ parents_____₁₅ car?

MARIO: Oh, no. _____₁₆ is an old Fiat. That's _____₁₇ sister _____₁₈ car.

UNIT 8

1 Rick is studying about Marco Polo in his history class. Look at the pictures and read the sentences. The pictures are in the correct order, but the sentences aren't. Number the sentences in the correct order.

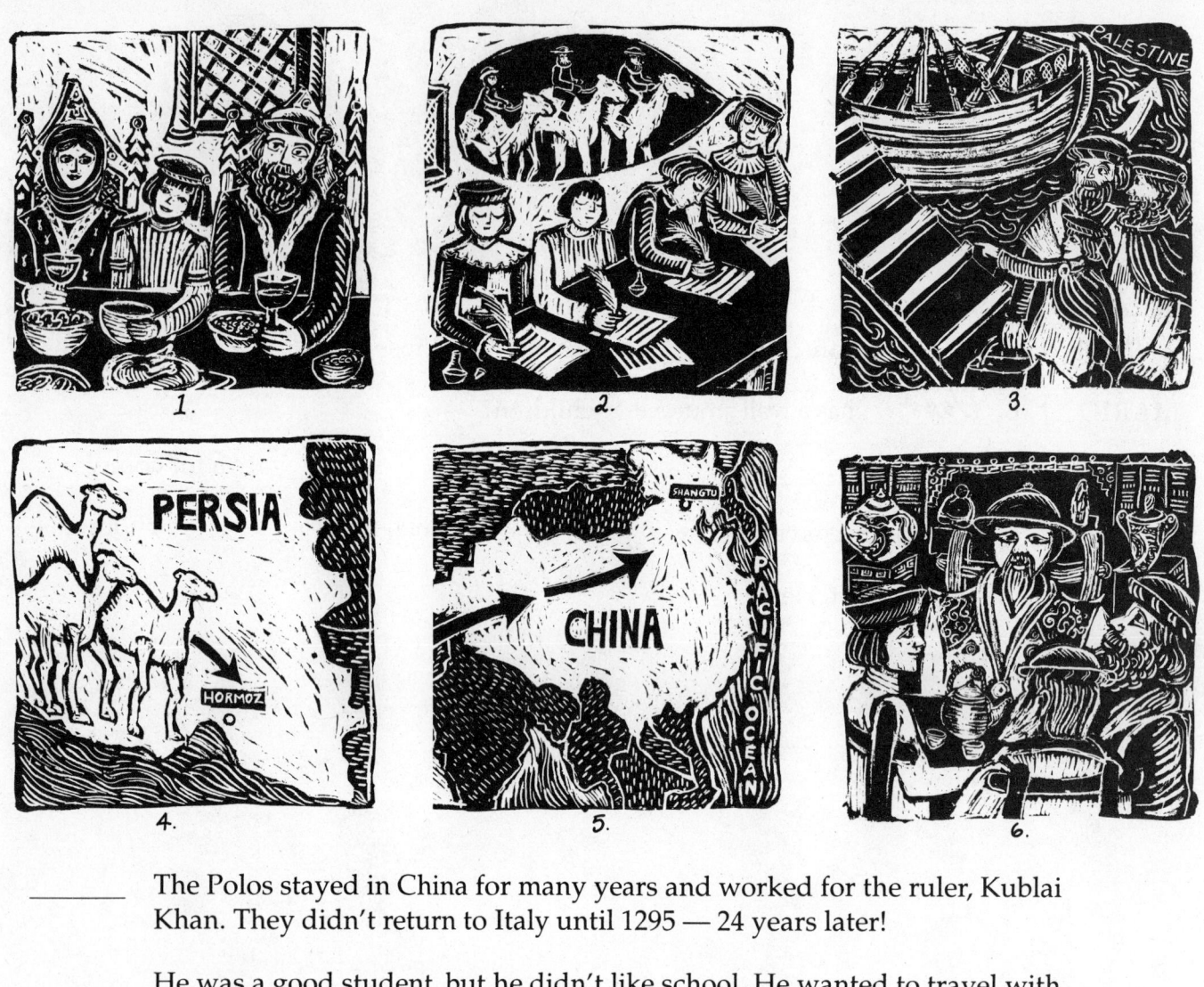

_____ The Polos stayed in China for many years and worked for the ruler, Kublai Khan. They didn't return to Italy until 1295 — 24 years later!

_____ He was a good student, but he didn't like school. He wanted to travel with his father.

__1__ Marco Polo, a famous traveler and explorer, was born in Venice, Italy, around 1254. When he was young, he lived with his aunt and uncle because his father traveled a lot and his mother was dead.

_____ Then they rode camels to Persia (now Iran). They wanted to sail to China from there, but there weren't any good ships.

_____ In 1271 Marco left Venice with his father, Nicolo, and his uncle Maffeo. First, they sailed to Palestine.

_____ So they traveled by camel across Asia to China. It took three years.

2 *Use the sentences in Exercise 1 (page 50) to write three paragraphs about Marco Polo.*

Marco Polo, a famous traveler and adventurer,

3 *Ann Daly is talking on the phone with her friend Linda. Complete the conversation with the past tense of the verbs in parentheses. Choose the correct forms from the words in the box. You may want to use some words more than once.*

wanted	weren't	called	talked
loved	left	went	didn't have
were	got	had	didn't get
was			

ANN: Hi, Linda. I *called* (1. call) you last week, but you _____ (2. be, neg.) home.

LINDA: I know. I _____ (3. be) in China.

ANN: You're kidding!

LINDA: No, really. We just _____ (4. get) home last night. It _____ (5. be) wonderful!

ANN: I'm sure it _____ (6. be). Frank and Alice _____ (7. go) to Beijing last year. They _____ (8. love) it. I think they _____ (9. be) in Shanghai too.

LINDA: I know. I _____ (10. talk) to Alice before I _____ (11. leave). We _____ (12. be) there too, but we also _____ (13. go) to central China. We _____ (14. want) to follow part of Marco Polo's trail.

ANN: How interesting!

LINDA: We _____ (15. get, neg.) to go everywhere, but it _____ (16. be) great. I _____ (17. have) a wonderful time. But poor Harry _____ (18. have, neg.) much fun.

ANN: No?

LINDA: No. He _____ (19. be) sick most of the time.

ANN: How awful!

GRAMMAR BOX

Past Tense – Affirmative and Negative

be

Affirmative (+)	Negative (-)
I was	wasn't
you were	weren't
he, she, it was	wasn't
we were	weren't
you were	weren't
they were	weren't

Irregular Verb Forms

become	became	didn't become
eat	ate	didn't eat
fly	flew	didn't fly
get	got	didn't get
give	gave	didn't give
go	went	didn't go
have	had	didn't have
know	knew	didn't know
leave	left	didn't leave
meet	met	didn't meet
ride	rode	didn't ride
spend	spent	didn't spend
take	took	didn't take
think	thought	didn't think
write	wrote	didn't write

Regular Verb – *want*

I wanted	didn't want
you wanted	didn't want
he, she, it wanted	didn't want
we wanted	didn't want
you wanted	didn't want
they wanted	didn't want

A: Where were you last night?
B: I went to the movies.
A: Did you go alone?
B: Yes, but I met John there.

---

4 *Choose a word or expression from each of the columns and write as many sentences as you can. Use a separate sheet of paper if necessary.*

Marco Polo	were	Italians.
Marco's aunt and uncle	was	an Italian.
Nicolo and Maffeo Polo	wasn't	the ruler of Cathay.
The Kublai Khan	weren't	merchants.
		an explorer.

1. Marco Polo was an Italian.
2. _____
3. _____
4. _____
5. _____
6. _____
7. _____

5 *This is a page from Rick's history textbook. Complete the paragraphs with the past tense of the verbs in parentheses.*

Marco Polo _____ a book about his travels.
(1. write)

The book _____ a best-seller all over Europe, but most people _____
(2. become) (3. believe, *neg.*)

that it was true. At that time, Europeans _____ a postal system;
(4. have, *neg.*)

they _____ paper money; they _____ coal
(5. use, *neg.*) (6. use, *neg.*)

for fuel; and they _____ about printing, gunpowder,
(7. know, *neg.*)

umbrellas, or spaghetti. Marco Polo _____
(8. tell)

them about these things in China.

The Chinese _____ a very good postal system; they _____ how to
(9. have) (10. know)

print and how to make gunpowder; they _____ noodles (spaghetti); and they
(11. eat)

_____ paper money, umbrellas, and coal. Marco Polo _____ the coal
(12. use) (13. call)

"black stones." The Europeans _____ this _____ impossible. The
(14. think) (15. be)

Chinese _____ Christian. It _____ impossible for
(16. be, *neg.*) (17. be)

them to know things that the Europeans _____ !
(18. know, *neg.*)

Now you're ready for the computer. When you finish at the computer, go to page 55.

6 Read the letter from Ann's mother. Then write the letter again. Change the verbs to the past tense.

> Our vacation is all planned. We leave here Sunday, and Betty meets us at the plane in Honolulu. She flies with us to Maui, and we spend two or three days in a beautiful little hotel on the beach there. Then Roger, Betty's husband, joins us on Friday, but he doesn't want to stay in Hawaii. He only has one week's vacation, and he doesn't want to spend it on the beach. So he and Betty go to Tokyo on Saturday morning.
> Your father just wants to relax, so we stay in Maui another week. The little hotel has a beautiful pool and a wonderful restaurant, so we don't have to move for two weeks.

Our vacation was lovely. We left here Sunday,

7 *When Marco Polo first saw the palace of the Kublai Khan, this is what he thought. Read the description.*

The Kublai Khan has a beautiful marble palace. It faces the city, and the back of the palace is against a huge wall. The wall surrounds the palace, the city, and sixteen miles of gardens, parks, and rivers. Many of the rooms in the palace are covered with gold. This is the Khan's summer palace. He stays there only in June, July, and August.

All kinds of animals and birds live in the parks. Some of them are wild; others are not. There are also about 10,000 beautiful white horses. These horses give milk, and this is the milk that the royal family drinks.

8 *After Marco Polo left the Kublai Khan, he wrote the description again —in the past. Write the paragraphs in Exercise 7 on page 56 again. Change the verbs to the past tense.*

The Kublai Khan had a beautiful

UNIT 9

1 *This is another page from Rick's history textbook. Read about Pompeii.*

Pompeii was a beautiful little town of about 20,000 people. It was in the south of Italy, not far from the Mediterranean Sea and about a mile from the volcano, Vesuvius. It was a busy town full of houses, shops, markets, bars, public baths, and theaters. The streets were always noisy and crowded with people and animals.

One day, in the summer of 79 A.D., Vesuvius erupted. Hot ashes and poisonous gases came out of the volcano. The wind carried the ash and gas toward the Mediterranean and toward Pompeii. The people in the town heard the eruption. They saw the ash, and they smelled the gas. A lot of them left the city by boat. Some escaped by land. But many people did not get out. They breathed the gas and died. The eruption lasted for several days. More and more ash came out of Vesuvius. It covered the whole city of Pompeii.

2 *Answer the questions about Pompeii. If you can't find the answers in the paragraphs on page 58, write **I don't know**.*

1. Where was Pompeii? *In the south of Italy.*

2. Was Pompeii near the Mediterranean? _____

3. Was Pompeii a quiet little town? _____

4. Were there theaters in Pompeii? _____

5. Were there movie theaters? _____

6. How many people lived in Pompeii? _____

7. What was the name of the volcano? _____

8. When did the volcano erupt? _____

9. What did people see after the eruption? _____

10. What did they smell? _____

11. How did people leave Pompeii after the eruption? _____

12. Who left? _____

13. Where did they go? _____

14. Did everyone leave? _____

15. How many people died in Pompeii? _____

16. Why did they die? _____

17. How long did the eruption last? _____

18. Did people come back to live in Pompeii after the eruption? _____

GRAMMAR BOX

Questions — Simple Past

Notice how questions are formed:

a. with the verb *to be*

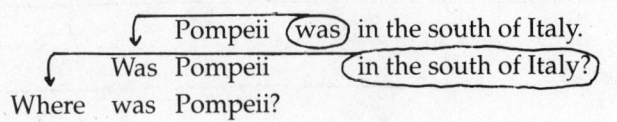

    Pompeii was in the south of Italy.
    Was Pompeii in the south of Italy?
  Where was Pompeii?

b. with other verbs

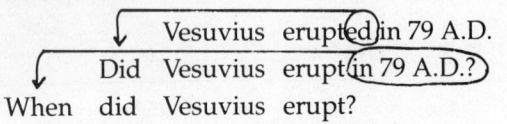

    Vesuvius erupted in 79 A.D.
    Did Vesuvius erupt in 79 A.D.?
  When did Vesuvius erupt?

A: Did you see that?
B: No. What was it?
A: I don't know. There was something strange in the sky.
B: What did it look like? Did it have wings?

A: It had an unusual shape.
B: Was it a UFO?
A: Maybe!

---

3 Look at the map of one part of Pompeii. Then complete the questions on page 61 with *was, were,* or *did* and answer each question with a short answer. If you don't know the answer, write **I don't know**.

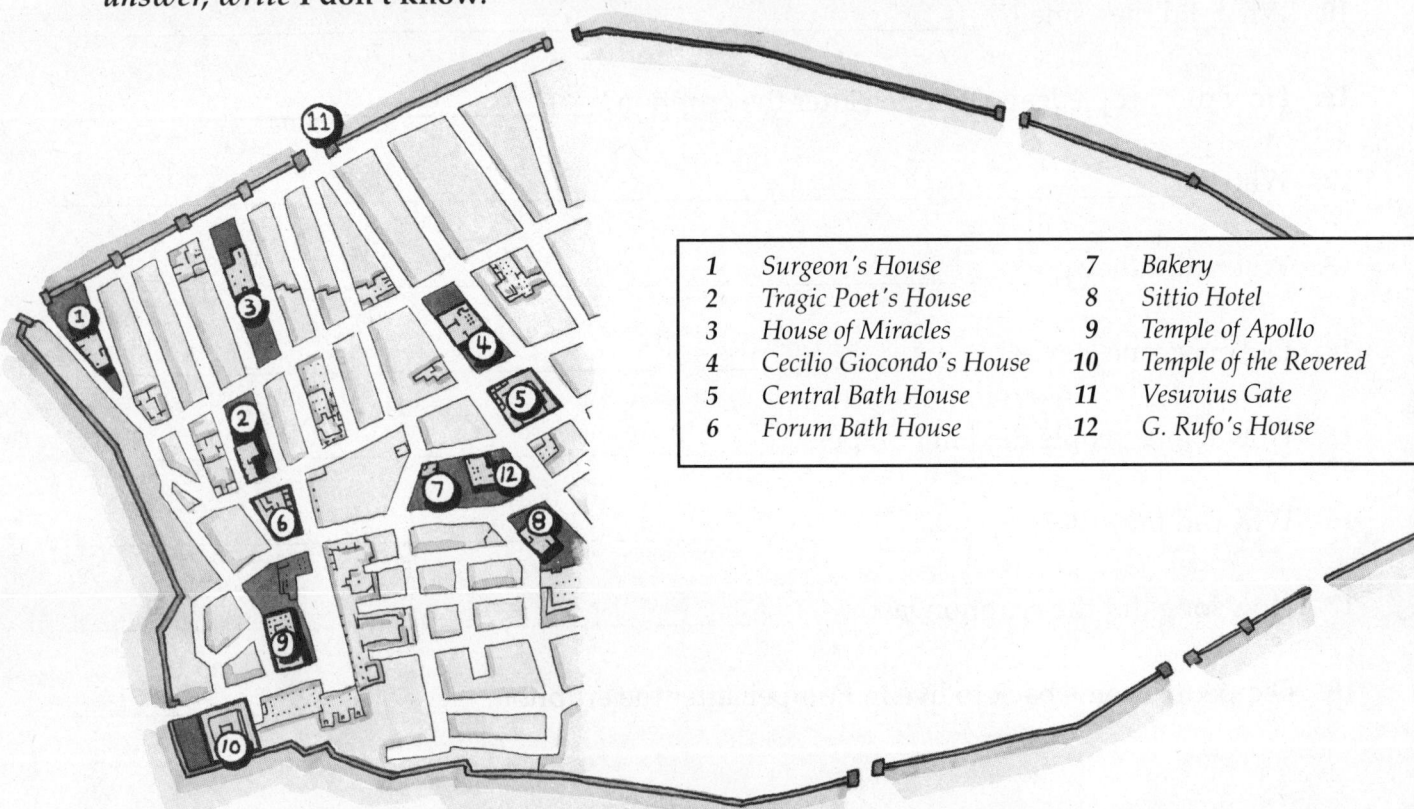

1	Surgeon's House	7	Bakery
2	Tragic Poet's House	8	Sittio Hotel
3	House of Miracles	9	Temple of Apollo
4	Cecilio Giocondo's House	10	Temple of the Revered
5	Central Bath House	11	Vesuvius Gate
6	Forum Bath House	12	G. Rufo's House

1. _Were_ there bath houses in Pompeii? _Yes, there were._
2. _____ there any temples? _____
3. _____ the surgeon's house near the Vesuvius Gate? _____
4. _____ the people live in tents? _____
5. _____ there any restaurants in this part of Pompeii? _____
6. _____ the Vesuvius Gate near the Temple of the Revered? _____
7. _____ Cecilio Giocondo have a house in Pompeii? _____
8. _____ Sophia Loren have a house there? _____
9. _____ there a hotel or inn in Pompeii? _____

4 Look again at the map of Pompeii on page 60. Then complete the questions with **what, where,** or **who** and answer the questions.

1. _____ lived in number 12?
   _____

2. _____ did the tragic poet live?
   _____

3. _____ did people do in 5 and 6?
   _____

4. _____ did the person in number 1 do?
   _____

5. _____ did the people at number 7 do?
   _____

5 Rick is still studying about Pompeii in his history class. He and the other students are asking the teacher questions. Complete the conversation with the words in parentheses. Be sure to use the correct past-tense form of the verb.

RICK: What _____ their houses like?
(1. be)

TEACHER: Most of the houses _____ two stories. The first floor _____ a shop,
(2. have) (3. be)

and the people _____ on the second floor.
(4. live)

ELLEN: _____ churches?
(5. they/have)

TEACHER: No. They _____ temples.
(6. have)

ALAN: What _____?
(7. they/eat)

TEACHER: Well, we think they _____ olives, bread, cheese, things like that. It's
(8. eat)

interesting too. They probably _____ down to eat!
(9. lie)

SUSAN: _____ there schools?
(10. be)

TEACHER: Not like our schools. Boys _____ classes, but girls didn't.
(11. have)

RICK: What _____?
(12. they/study)

TEACHER: We're not sure, but probably Latin, math, history, and geography.

STEVE: How many people _____ when Vesuvius erupted?
(13. die)

TEACHER: At least 200.

ELLEN: How _____?
(14. the other people/escape)

TEACHER: A lot of them _____ away in boats.
(15. get)

RICK: Where _____?
(16. they/go)

TEACHER: I don't know.

ALAN: When _____ Pompeii?
(17. they/discover)

TEACHER: Well, the King of Naples _____ to dig there in 1748.
(18. start)

RICK: So Pompeii _____ buried almost 1,700 years! Incredible!
(19. be)

Now you're ready for the computer. When you finish at the computer, go to page 63.

6 Complete the conversation with the words in parentheses. Be sure to use the correct past-tense form of the verb.

ANN: *Where did you go on your vacation*_____?
(1. where/you/go/on your vacation)

SUE: I _____ to Italy.
(2. go)

ANN: Really? _____?
(3. you/like/it)

SUE: I _____ it.
(4. love)

ANN: Yes, it's a beautiful country.

SUE: _____?
(5. when/you/be/there)

ANN: A couple of years ago. We _____ to the south: Rome, Naples, Pompeii...
(6. go)

SUE: _____?
(7. how/you/like/Naples)

ANN: It _____ wonderful.
(8. be)

SUE: I _____ it too, but the children _____ Rome more.
(9. love) (10. like)

ANN: Oh, _____?
(11. they/be/with you)

SUE: Yes.

ANN: _____?
(12. Frank/go/too)

SUE: Of course.

ANN: _____?
(13. what/he/like/best)

SUE: Oh, he _____ Pompeii.
(14. love)

ANN: _____?
(15. your guide/be/good)

SUE: No. He _____ very much, but we _____ a good book.
(16. know, *neg.*) (17. have)

ANN: _____?
(18. he/show/you/the graffiti on the amphitheater)

SUE: Yes. _____ it interesting?
(19. be, *neg.*)

ANN: _____?
(20. you/stay in Naples)

SUE: Yes. We _____ there for two nights. It _____ great!
(21. stay) (22. be)

7 *Pretend that you are going to interview a famous person who is dead now. Read the examples. Then write four or five questions that you are going to ask the person you chose to interview.*

Questions that I want to ask Marilyn Monroe:
- Where were you born?
- When did you first become famous?
- Why were you unhappy?
- Which husband did you like the best?
- How did you die?

Questions that I want to ask _____:

1. _____
2. _____
3. _____
4. _____
5. _____

UNIT 10

1 *Read the sentences. Then look at the pictures and write the correct sentence under each picture.*

- They built it two years ago.
- She loves him, but does he love her?
- Bert loves one of them, but which one?
- Kathleen and Diane's mother gave them these diamonds, but Kathleen has them now.

1. Bert and Diane are married. _____

2. Kathleen and Diane are sisters. _____

3. _____

4. This is Bert and Diane's boat house.

Now write these sentences in the correct balloons.

- Bert, do you love me?
- I can't love you, Kathleen.
- Bert, Kathleen loves you. Do you love her?

5. *I can't love you, Kathleen.* I'm married to Diane.

6.

GRAMMAR BOX

Object Pronouns

I → me	we → us
you → you	you → you
he → him	they → them
she → her	
it → it	

A: How was your trip to Brazil?
B: It was great!
A: Were your relatives happy to see you?
B: They were thrilled to see me — especially with my family. They fed us constantly. I gained ten pounds!
A: Did Mary enjoy the trip too?
B: Well, she doesn't speak Portuguese, so it was a little difficult for her. But Danny had a wonderful time. My mother and all my aunts tried to teach him Portuguese, and he tried to teach them English.

---

2 *Read this sentence:* **I remember John, but he doesn't remember me.**
Now write the sentence again. Change the first word each time and make all the other necessary changes.

1. Maryann
   Maryann remembers John, but he doesn't remember her.

2. The Franklins

3. My wife and I

4. Jeff

5. You

6. You and Kate

3 *Read the conversation. Then look at the pictures and write the conversation again. Change **Linda** to the words given and make all the other necessary changes.*

A: Did you find Linda?
B: Yes.
A: Where did you find her?
B: In the backyard.

1. your shoes

   A: *Did you find your shoes?*
   B: _____
   A: _____
   B: _____

2. your sister

   A: _____
   B: _____
   A: _____
   B: _____

3. your key

   A: _____
   B: _____
   A: _____
   B: _____

4. your brother

   A: _____
   B: _____
   A: _____
   B: _____

5. your dog

   A: _____
   B: _____
   A: _____
   B: _____

4 Amy and her friends are talking about a popular TV show. Complete the conversation with me, you, him, her, them, us, or it.

JANE: What happened on *Houston* last night?

AMY: I don't know. I missed _____.
                                   1

JANE: But I asked _____ to watch _____!
                      2   3

BILL: Don't worry, ladies. I saw _____.
                                   4

JANE: Well, what happened?

BILL: Do you remember last week, when Bert and Diane stole Kathleen's diamonds and hid _____ in their boat house? Well, this week two men broke into Bert and
           5
Diane's house.

AMY: Of course Kathleen sent _____.
                                6

BILL: Of course. Well, they looked all over for the diamonds, but they didn't find _____.
                                                                                      7

JANE: Were Bert and Diane home? Did the robbers find _____?
                                                         8

BILL: Yes. They were in bed. Bert yelled, "Don't come near _____."
                                                               9

JANE: What did the robbers do to _____?
                                    10

BILL: Well, they tied Bert up and left _____ in the house, and they took
                                          11
Diane with _____.
               12

AMY: Did they tie _____ up too?
                      13

BILL: No, and she screamed, "Please don't hurt _____! Please don't hurt _____!"
                                                   14   15
about a hundred times. But the robbers didn't pay any attention to _____.
                                                                       16

AMY: Did she tell _____ where to find the diamonds?
                      17

BILL: Of course. And then they tied _____ up and left _____ in the boat house.
                                        18   19

JANE: So did Bert and Diane get away?

BILL: Watch next week and find out.

Now you're ready for the computer. When you finish at the computer, go to page 69.

5 *Look at the pictures and use the words to write conversations. Follow the example in number 1.*

1. I/shoes/mother

   A: *I have some new shoes.*
   B: *Where did you get them?*
   A: *My mother gave them to me.*

2. David/watch/dad

   A: _____
   B: _____
   A: _____

3. Jenny and Tony/refrigerator/parents

   A: _____
   B: _____
   A: _____

4. I/bicycle/brother

   A: _____
   B: _____
   A: _____

5. Frank and I/car/children

   A: _____
   B: _____
   A: _____

6. Mary/skis/husband

   A: _____
   B: _____
   A: _____

6 *This is part of a letter. Read the paragraph. Then write the paragraph again. Change* **Linda** *to the words given and make all the other necessary changes.*

> Linda just got a new car, and it's beautiful. Her parents gave it to her for her birthday. She drove it yesterday for the first time.

1. the MacDonald twins

2. Frank

3. I

4. Jack and I (*also change* parents *to* children *and* birthday *to* anniversary)

UNIT 11

1 *Pretend that you are the silhouette in the picture. You are directing and acting in a play. You are showing another actor a picture of the first scene, and you are telling him about it. Read the sentences. Then look at the picture and write the correct letter in each blank.*

a. David, you and I are sitting in the living room. We're watching TV.
b. They're both wearing party hats too.
c. Dick and Marjorie are standing outside the door.
d. Marjorie is holding a cake.
e. I'm knitting.
f. Dick is holding a big box and some balloons.
g. You're smoking a pipe.
h. There's a cat under my chair. It's sleeping—we hope.

2 *Pretend that you are talking to the director of the play in Exercise 1. Look again at the picture on page 71 and answer the questions with short answers.*

1. Is David standing up? __No, he isn't.__
2. Are you watching TV? _____
3. Is Dick watching TV too? _____
4. Is the cat eating its dinner? _____
5. Are Dick and Marjorie looking in the window? _____
6. Is Marjorie standing in front of Dick? _____
7. Is Dick wearing shorts? _____
8. Are you and David sitting in the living room? _____

3 *Here is another scene from the play in Exercise 1. Pretend that you are the silhouette and you are acting and directing. David is asking you questions. Look at the picture. Then answer the questions with the correct sentences from the box on page 73.*

1. Where am I?
   __You're standing at the head of the table.__

2. What am I doing?
   _____

3. Where are you sitting?
   _____

4. What are you and Marjorie doing?
   _____

5. Where is Dick standing?
   _____

6. What's he doing?
   _____

> - We're clapping.
> - He's taking a picture of us.
> - You're blowing out the candles.
> - You're standing at the head of the table.
> - I'm sitting across from Marjorie.
> - He's standing at the kitchen door.

GRAMMAR BOX

Present Progressive

			Short Answers	
Affirmative (+)	**Interrogative (?)**	**Negative (–)**	**(+)**	**(–)**
I'm playing	am I playing	I'm not playing	Yes, I am.	No, I'm not.
you're playing	are you playing	you aren't playing	Yes, you are.	No, you aren't.
he's playing	is he playing	he isn't playing	Yes, he is.	No, he isn't.
she's playing	is she playing	she isn't playing	Yes, she is.	No, she isn't.
it's playing	is it playing	it isn't playing	Yes, it is.	No, it isn't.
we're playing	are we playing	we aren't playing	Yes, we are.	No, we aren't.
you're playing	are you playing	you aren't playing	Yes, you are.	No, you aren't.
they're playing	are they playing	they aren't playing	Yes, they are.	No, they aren't.

SOME SPELLING RULES: If a verb ends in *e*, drop the *e* before you add *–ing*: take → taking.
If a verb ends in consonant + vowel + consonant, double the last consonant before you add *–ing*: shop → shopping.

+			Tom (is) visiting his sister today.
?		Is	Tom visiting his sister today?
–	No,		he isn't visiting his sister today.
?	Who	is	Tom visiting today?

A: Mom, I'm having trouble with my homework. Can you help me?
B: I'm sorry, dear. I can't help you now. I'm cooking dinner. What's your sister doing?
A: She's talking on the phone.
B: Well, tell her to hang up now. Then she can help you.

4 Look at the pictures and use the words to describe what the people are doing. Pretend that you are the silhouette.

1. Daniel/work
   Daniel is working.

2. Fanny/study
   _____

3. Kay and Al/clean/the house
   _____

4. you/do (*neg.*)/it right
   _____

5. Jim and I/play/tennis
   _____

6. I/hit/the ball
   _____

5 Complete the questions with the correct present–progressive form of the verb in parentheses. Then look again at the pictures in Exercise 4 and answer the questions. If you don't know the answer, write **I don't know**. Use contractions when you can.

1. What **'s** Daniel **doing**? (do)
   He's working.

2. Where _____ Daniel _____? (go)
   _____

3. _____ Daniel _____ a tie? (wear)

4. Where _____ Fanny _____? (study)

5. _____ she _____ history? (study)

6. Who _____ _____ the floor? (mop)

7. What _____ Al _____? (do)

8. _____ Al and Kay _____ the bedroom? (clean)

9. _____ you _____ the diaper? (change)

10. What _____ the baby _____? (do)

11. Who _____ _____ tennis? (play)

12. _____ you and Jim _____ bathing suits? (wear)

Now you're ready for the computer. When you finish at the computer, go to page 76.

6 Ann and Bob are at their 20th college reunion. They're talking to two of their old classmates. Write questions and statements with the words in parentheses. Be sure to use the correct form of the present progressive.

ANN: _____?
(1. what/you and Beth/do/now)

JOE: _____.
(2. Beth/teach/high school, and I/work, neg.)

ANN: _____?
(3. what/you/do)

JOE: I'm in school. _____.
(4. I/study/nursing)

ANN: Really? That's wonderful! _____?
(5. you/still/live/here)

BETH: No. _____.
(6. we/live/in Nebraska now)

_____?
(7. where/you and Bob/live)

ANN: _____.
(8. we/live, neg./here anymore either)

_____.
(9. we/live/in Barker, Kansas)

7 Now Ann, Bob, Joe, and Beth are talking about other classmates. Write questions with the words in parentheses. Then look at the pictures and answer the questions.

ANN: _____?
(Linda Sue/still/work/for Shopwell)

BETH: _____

BOB: _____?
(what/she/do)

BETH: _____

JOE: What about Jim Garner? _____?
(he/still/teach)

ANN: No. _____

BOB: And you know that he married Chris Farley, don't you?

JOE: You're kidding! _____?
(where/they/live/now)

BOB: _____

76

UNIT 12

1 Look at the pictures. Then use the correct phrase to complete each sentence.

- she's skipping class today.
- his co-pilot is checking it now.
- this year they're traveling in China.

- she's sleeping now.
- she's spending this weekend at the lake.
- today Bob is working and Rick is studying.

1. Ann almost always gets up at 7:00, but _____

2. Amy almost never misses a class, but _____

3. Bob and Rick sometimes go fishing on Saturday, but _____

4. Ann's parents usually spend Thanksgiving with her, but _____

5. Ann often has to work on weekends, but _____

6. Bob almost always checks the plane before he takes off, but _____

77

2 *Read the examples. Then complete the sentences about yourself.*

I usually ___*write in Spanish*___, but I'm ___*writing in English*___ right now.

I usually ___*study English in the morning*___, and I'm ___*studying English*___ right now.

1. I usually _____, but I'm _____ right now.

2. I usually _____, and I'm _____ right now.

GRAMMAR BOX

**Simple Present vs. Present Progressive
Frequency Adverbs**

1. Use the present progressive for an action happening NOW: It's 8:30. Jane is getting up.
2. Use the simple present for an action that happens regularly: Jane gets up at 8:30 every morning.
3. Frequency adverbs

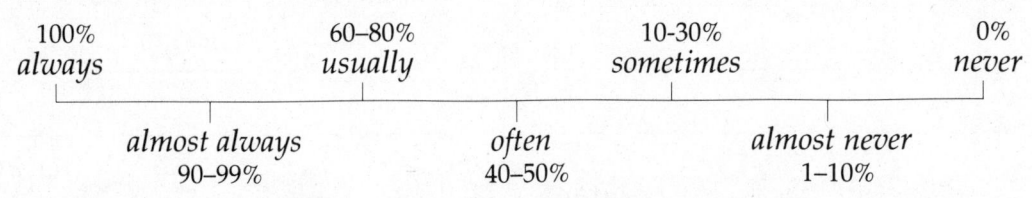

100%	60–80%	10-30%	0%
always	usually	sometimes	never
almost always 90–99%		often 40–50%	almost never 1–10%

Notice the placement of frequency adverbs: Jane always gets up at 8:30.
　　　　　　　　　　　　　　　　　　　　She often takes the bus to work.
　　　　　　　　　　　　　　　　　　　　She is almost always on time.

A: Look at Mary! She's running down the street!
B: Is someone running after her?
A: No, no one is running after her.
B: Why is she running then?
A: She runs for exercise.
B: Oh. How often does she run?
A: Three or four times a week. But she usually runs in the morning; she almost never runs at night.

3 Look at the statistics on the weather in Mexico City. Then complete the sentences with adverbs of frequency.

Chance of rain in June	95%	Chance of wind in February	65%
Chance of rain in December	5%	Chance of hot weather in March	90%
Chance of snow in winter	1%	Chance of cool weather in July	75%
Chance of hail in summer	20%		

1. It _____ rains in June.
2. It _____ rains in December.
3. It _____ snows in the winter.
4. It _____ hails in the summer.
5. It's _____ windy in February.
6. It's _____ hot in March.
7. It's _____ cool in July.

4 Answer the questions. You don't have to use complete sentences.

1. What do you usually do on weekends? _____
2. How often do you go to the movies? _____
3. How often do you watch TV? _____
4. Do you and your family eat in restaurants very often? _____
5. What's something you never do? _____
6. Do you always get to work (school) on time? _____
7. What are you doing right now? _____
8. What are you wearing today? _____

Now you're ready for the computer. When you finish at the computer, go to page 80.

5 Complete the phone conversations with the words in parentheses. Be sure to use the correct form of the verb: either the simple present or the present progressive.

1. **A:** Hi, Ellie. What _____ (you/do)?
   B: _____ (I/read) the newspaper.

2. **A:** Where's Jimmy?
   B: _____ (I/know, neg.).
   _____ (he/usually/get, neg.) home until after 7:00 on Fridays.

3. **A:** Is Pete there?
   B: Yes, he is. But _____ (he/take) a shower right now.

4. **A:** I'm sorry to bother you. _____ (you/eat) dinner?
   B: No. _____ (we/never/eat) until 7:00.

5. **A:** How often _____ (you/go) to the movies?
   B: _____ (I/love) movies, so _____ (I/usually/go) about twice a week. But this week _____ (I/work) nights, so I can't go.

6. **A:** _____ (Debbie/study) for her history test?
   B: No. _____ (she/never/study) after 10:00.

7. **A:** Where are your parents?
   B: _____ (they/visit) my grandmother in Florida. _____ (they/always/spend) a week with her in January.

8. **A:** _____ (you/ever/go out) for lunch on Sunday?
   B: No. _____ (I/almost always/get up) late, so _____ (I/read) the newspaper and then _____ (I/go) to the little coffee shop on the corner for coffee.

6 Look at Stephanie's calendar. Then write as many sentences as you can with these frequency adverbs: always, almost always, usually, sometimes, almost never, never.

Sun.	Mon.	Tues.	Wed.	Thurs.	Fri.	Sat.
MAY	1 Work 9-5	2 Work 9-5	3 Work 9-5	4 Work 9-5 Take Karate 7	5 Work 9-5	6 Go to the movies with Pete
7 Take Mom to Church	8 Work 4-11	9 Work 9-5	10 Work 9-5	11 Work 9-5 Take Karate 7	12 Work 9-5	13
14 Go out to lunch w/ Gayle Go Swimming	15 Work 4-11	16 Work 9-5	17 Work 9-5	18 Work 9-5 Take Karate 7	19 Work 9-5	20 Go to the movies with Dan
21 Take Mom to Church Go Swimming	22 Watch Music Special Channel 12 8	23 Work 9-5	24 Work 9-5	25 Work 9-5 Take Karate 7	26 Work 4-11	27 Work 4-11
28 Take Mom to Church	29 Work 9-5	30 Work 9-5				

1. Stephanie always takes a karate class on Thursday night.
2. _____
3. _____
4. _____
5. _____
6. _____
7. _____
8. _____

7 *Look at the pictures. Then look again at Stephanie's calendar on page 81. Write sentences about the things that Stephanie is doing this May.*

Mon., May 8

1. *Stephanie sometimes works 9-5 on Monday, but today (and next Monday) she's working 4-11.*

Sat., May 13

2. _____

Sun., May 14

3. _____

Sat., May 27

4. _____

UNIT 13

1 Look at the pictures and match the two columns. Then write the complete sentences.

1. Owls can — see in the dark.
2. Camels can — go without water for several days.
3. The bat is the only mammal that can — fly.
4. Octopuses can — change color.
5. A gazelle can — jump 30 feet.
6. Salmon can — swim upstream.
7. Chimpanzees can — learn sign language.
8. Pelicans can — store fish in their pouches.

1. *Owls can see in the dark.*
2. _____
3. _____
4. _____
5. _____
6. _____
7. _____
8. _____

2 *Answer the questions with one of these short answers:* **Yes, I/he/she/we/they can** *or* **No, I/he/she/we/they can't.** *Then ask a friend the questions and write his or her answers.*

	Your answer	Your friend's answer
1. Can you drive?	_____	_____
2. Can you and your parents fly a plane?	_____	_____
3. Can your teacher speak English?	_____	_____
4. Can you speak Spanish?	_____	_____
5. Can your boyfriend/girlfriend/husband/wife cook?	_____	_____
6. Can your parents work a computer?	_____	_____

3 *Complete the conversation with* **what, where,** *or* **what time.**

LYNN: _____1_____ can we leave tomorrow?

JOHN: Is 4:30 OK?

LYNN: Sure. _____2_____ can we meet?

JOHN: Let's meet in front of the school.

LYNN: OK. And _____3_____ can you bring?

JOHN: I can bring fruit and iced tea. Can you bring some sandwiches?

LYNN: Of course. I'll see you tomorrow.

4 Read the sentences. Then look at the pictures and write the correct sentence under each picture.

- Can you turn down the radio, please?
- Can you get me a candy bar?

- Can you open the door, please?
- Can you close those windows?

1. _____

2. _____

3. _____

4. _____

5 Think of a friend or family member. Which of these questions would you ask him or her? How would he or she answer? Put a check (✓) next to the questions that you would ask. Then write an answer. You can answer with **Sure/OK/Of course/No/Absolutely not**.

1. **A:** Can I borrow $5.00?
   B: _____

2. **A:** Can I borrow the car?
   B: _____

3. **A:** Can I have another piece of cake?
   B: _____

4. **A:** Can your dog come out and play with me?
   B: _____

5. **A:** Can I use your pen?
   B: _____

6. **A:** Can I throw these shoes away?
   B: _____

GRAMMAR BOX

can

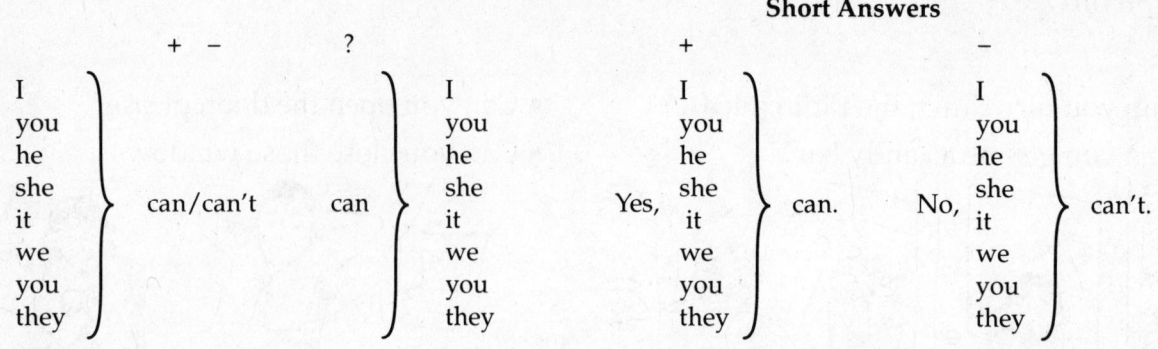

	+ −	?		Short Answers +	−
I you he she it we you they	can/can't	can { I you he she it we you they	Yes, { I you he she it we you they } can.	No, { I you he she it we you they } can't.

Use *can* to show:

1) ability: Tom is very tall. He can reach the book on the top shelf.
   Joe is short. He can't reach it.

2) permission: Yes, you can have a cookie. But remember, you can't go out until you finish your homework.

3) requests: Bob, I'm tired. Can you take the dog for a walk, please?

---

6 Look at the pictures of Bob, Rick, Amy, and Ann and Bob. Then write sentences with **can** or **can't** and the words given.

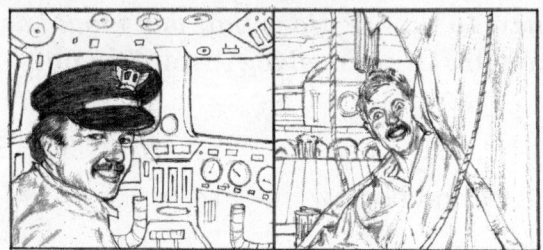

1. fly a plane/sail a boat

   Bob can fly a plane, but he can't sail a boat.

2. play the guitar/sing

   Rick _____

3. drive a car/ride a motorcycle

   Amy _____

4. play tennis/play golf

   Ann _____

7 *Pretend that you are going on a trip. Complete the requests that you might make to a friend.*

1. _____ water my plants?
2. _____ feed my cat?
3. _____ pick up my mail?
4. _____ take me to the airport?

Now write your own requests.

1. _____
2. _____
3. _____

8 *Choose a word or expression from each of the columns and write questions. Then answer the questions.*

How far		your parents	run
How fast	can	you	speak
What languages		your teacher	cook
What			read

1. _____?
   _____

2. _____?
   _____

3. _____?
   _____

4. _____?
   _____

Now you're ready for the computer. When you finish at the computer, go to page 88.

9 *Pretend that you are going to interview a famous person. Read the examples. Then write four or five questions with* **can** *that you would like to ask the person you chose to interview.*

Questions that I would like to ask Paul Newman:
Can you really ride a horse?
Can you sing?
Can you dance?

Questions that I would like to ask _____:

1. _____
2. _____
3. _____
4. _____
5. _____

10 *Look at the signs. Then write a sentence that tells what each sign means. Use* **can** *or* **can't** *in your sentences.*

1. *You can walk here.*

2. *You can't turn right here.*

3. _____

4. _____

5. _____ 6. _____

7. _____ 8. _____

11 *Complete the conversations with the words in parentheses. Use* **can** *in all your sentences.*

1. **A:** Excuse me. Where ___*can I buy*___ a map?
      (I/buy)

   B: I think _____ one at the gas station on the corner.
               (you/get)

2. **A:** Mom, _____ TV now?
               (I/watch)

   B: You know _____ TV. You have to study.
                  (you/watch, *neg.*)

3. **A:** Excuse me, miss. _____ that door?
                          (you/open)

   B: Certainly.

4. **A:** We need people for the talent show. _____?
                                               (Peter/sing)

   B: No, _____, but _____ and
            (he/sing, *neg.*)   (he/dance)
   _____.
   (he/play the piano)

UNIT 14

1 Mrs. Polenski won the lottery. Look at the pictures. Then put a check (✓) next to the sentences that you think she said to the reporters.

1. _____ My son is going to get a new car.
2. _____ My daughter is going to go to Gilford University.
3. _____ My daughter isn't going to have to go to school anymore.
4. _____ I'm going to stop working.
5. _____ I'm not going to stop working.
6. _____ My husband is going to be able to buy some new taxis.
7. _____ My parents are going to have a new house.
8. _____ My family and I are going to take a vacation in Hawaii.
9. _____ My family and I are going to build a swimming pool in the backyard.
10. _____ My family and I are going to move to New York City.

2 *Pretend that you are a reporter who interviewed Mrs. Polenski from Exercise 1. Your boss is asking you questions. Look again at the pictures on page 90 and answer the questions with short answers.*

1. Is Mrs. Polenski going to work eight hours a day from now on? *No, she isn't.*
2. Are she and her family going to take a vacation? _____
3. Is her son going to buy a new car? _____
4. Is her husband going to buy a new taxi? _____
5. Are her parents going to come and live with her? _____
6. Is her daughter going to stop studying? _____
7. Are the Polenskis going to move to New York? _____

Now answer these questions about yourself.

1. Are you going to buy a new car soon? _____
2. Are you and your family going to move this year? _____
3. Are you going to study English tonight? _____
4. Are you and your parents going to have dinner together tonight? _____
5. Are you going to take English next year? _____
6. Are you and your family going to watch TV tonight? _____
7. Are you going to read the newspaper tomorrow? _____

3 *Answer the questions about yourself, friends, and family. You don't have to write complete sentences. If you don't know the answer, write* **I don't know.**

1. What are you going to do when you finish this exercise?
   _____

2. What are you going to do tonight?
   _____

3. What's your brother (sister, mother, father, husband, wife, son, or daughter) going to do tonight?
   _____

4. When are you and a friend going to go out next?
   _____

5. When are you and your family going to go on your next vacation?
   _____

4 *This is a paragraph from a letter that Amy wrote to a friend on August 16th. Read about Amy and Rick's party.*

> August 16
>
> Dear Sally,
>
> Rick and I had a party on Friday the 13th. It was great! Everyone wore costumes. I dressed up like a black cat. Rick put on a cowboy hat and some old cowboy boots. Helen brought her record collection, so we had great music. We danced for hours; then we gave a prize for the best costume.

Write the paragraph in Exercise 4 on page 92 again. Pretend that Amy wrote the letter on August 9th, a week before the party. Change the verbs to the **going to** future.

Dear Sally, *August 9*

  Rick and I are going to have a

GRAMMAR BOX

Future with *going to*

Affirmative (+)	Interrogative (?)	Negative (−)
I'm going to play	am I going to play	I'm not going to play
you're going to play	are you going to play	you aren't going to play
he's going to play	is he going to play	he isn't going to play
she's going to play	is she going to play	she isn't going to play
it's going to play	is it going to play	it isn't going to play
we're going to play	are we going to play	we aren't going to play
you're going to play	are you going to play	you aren't going to play
they're going to play	are they going to play	they aren't going to play

NOTE: The short answers for the future with *going to* are the same as those for the present progressive.

Notice how the negative and questions are formed:

```
+        Jim  is       going to study medicine when he finishes college.
?        Is   Jim      going to study medicine when he finishes college?
?  What  is   Jim      going to study?
−             He isn't going to study law.
```

A: What are you going to do for vacation this summer?
B: Well, I'm not going to stay home this year! I'm going to visit my relatives in Italy. What about you? Are you going to go back to that place in Canada?
A: No. I'm going to travel around the States. Sue is going to come with me. We're both going to take three weeks off.

5 *Look at the pictures. Then write sentences about what the members of the Daly family are going to do on their next vacation.*

1. _____ 2. _____

3. _____

Now write a sentence about what you are going to do on your next vacation and a sentence about what you and your family (or you and a friend) are going to do.

1. _____
2. _____

6 *Write questions with the words in parentheses. Then look at the pictures in Exercise 5 and answer the questions. Use the **going to** future in both your questions and your answers.*

1. _____?
   (Rick/take/his sunglasses to camp)
   _____

2. _____?
   (he/take/his dog)
   _____

3. _____?
   (what/he/play)
   _____

4. _____?
   (how/Amy/get to Mexico)
   _____

5. _____?
   (who/she/go/with)

   _____

6. _____?
   (where/Ann and Bob/go)

   _____

7. _____?
   (they/take/their vacation in the summer or in the winter)

   _____

These questions are for you to answer about your vacation.

1. _____?
   (how/you/travel)

   _____

2. _____?
   (you/go/alone)

   _____

3. _____?
   (where/you (you and_____) /go)

   _____

4. _____?
   (what/you/do)

   _____

7 Write questions that you want to ask a friend about his or her next vacation.

1. _____

2. _____

3. _____

4. _____

Now you're ready for the computer. When you finish at the computer, go to page 96.

8 Complete the article from the Barker News with the correct form of the verb in parentheses. Use the simple past or the going to future.

BARKER NEWS
CHILD ACTRESS VISITS NEW YORK

Glenda Ford ____*arrived*____ in New York
      (1. arrive)
last night with her parents. The 8-year-old star of the
hit TV show Nelly ____*is going to attend*____ the
                        (2. attend)
opening of her new movie on Friday. She
_____ to the party after the
(3. go, neg.)
opening, however. "That's after her bedtime," her
mother _____.
         (4. say)
On Saturday Glenda and her parents _____ the mayor of New York,
                                        (5. visit)
and on Sunday afternoon she _____ out the prizes at the New York
                                (6. give)
Marathon. "I hope that the people in New York _____ my movie,"
                                                   (7. like)
Glenda _____. "I _____ a lot of fun making it."
         (8. say)   (9. have)

9 *Ann is talking to her father, Bill, who is going to go to Puerto Rico on a business trip. Write questions with the words in parentheses. Then read Bill's itinerary and answer the questions.*

Itinerary – Trip to San Juan (September 9–21) — Mr. & Mrs. Leak

Sept. 9	Leave for San Juan at 2:30 P.M. Arrive in San Juan at 7:30 P.M. Jeff Stone and Rita Morales, our representatives there, meet you. Transport to La Concha Hotel.	Sept. 10–12 Sept. 13–14 Sept. 14 Sept. 15–20 Sept. 21	Visits to factories in the San Juan area. FREE Mrs. Leak returns to Kansas City at 5:00 P.M. Visits to factories outside of San Juan. Return to Kansas City at 10:00 A.M.

ANN: Hi, Dad. How are you?

BILL: Great, Ann. And you?

ANN: Oh, I'm fine. _____?
(1. when/you/go/to San Juan)

BILL: _____

ANN: _____?
(2. how long/you/be gone)

BILL: _____

ANN: _____?
(3. Mom/go/with you)

BILL: _____

ANN: _____?
(4. she/stay/the whole time)

BILL: _____

ANN: Oh, _____?
(5. where/you/stay)

BILL: _____

ANN: _____?
(6. the company representatives/meet you)

BILL: _____

ANN: _____?
(7. what/you/do)

BILL: _____

ANN: _____?
(8. what/Mom/do)

BILL: Oh, lie on the beach, play tennis...

ANN: That sounds like fun. Can I go too?

UNIT 15

REVIEW OF VERBS

1 *Look at the pictures and read the paragraphs. The pictures show the story of Phil Kenshaw's life. The sentences tell the same story, but they aren't in the correct order. Write the sentences in each of the three paragraphs in the correct order.*

MR. BIOLOGY

"By the time I was ten, I knew I wanted to be a biologist."

•

"My mother didn't like animals," he told us, "but I loved them. I nearly drove her crazy."

•

Phil Kenshaw, Barker High's favorite biology teacher, was born right here in Barker, Kansas.

•

Before he was five, he had two dogs, a cat, a canary, five fish, and a hamster.

•

Now he is studying paleontology. "I study old bones," he said. "You know, dinosaurs, birds with teeth, fossils, things like that."

•

But he never stopped studying.

•

Phil Kenshaw, Barker High's favorite biology teacher, was born right here in Barker, Kansas.

Mr. Kenshaw began teaching biology soon after college.

•

Two days a week he goes to Lawrence and takes a class at the university there. He's working on his second PhD.

•

And how long is he going to go on teaching?

•

"I'm never going to stop studying or teaching," he said. "I'm 70 now, and I'm going to be teaching biology when I'm 90."

•

2 *Read the story in Exercise 1 (pages 98 and 99) again. Then answer these questions. Use complete sentences in your answers. If you can't find the answer, write I don't know.*

1. When was Phil Kenshaw born?

2. What town does he teach in?

3. What does he teach?

4. How many animals did he have when he was five?

5. Did he decide to become a biologist before or after he graduated from high school?

6. Is Phil studying for a PhD in education?

7. How often does he have classes in Lawrence?

8. How many PhD's does he have?

9. What is paleontology?

10. Is Phil still studying about animals?

11. When is Phil going to retire?

12. Is he going to teach paleontology when he gets his PhD?

3 Complete the conversation. Choose the correct answer and write it in the blank.

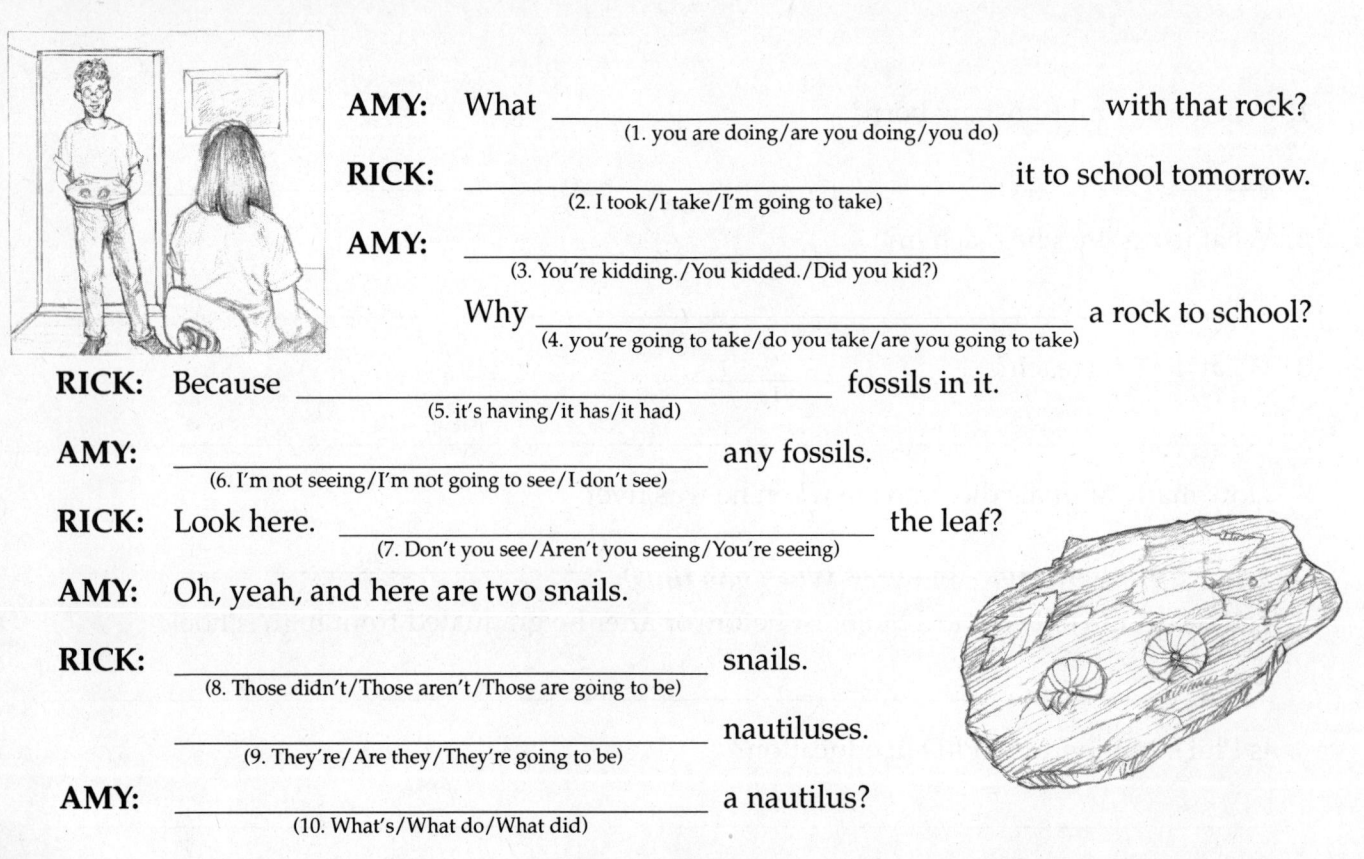

AMY: What _____ with that rock?
(1. you are doing/are you doing/you do)

RICK: _____ it to school tomorrow.
(2. I took/I take/I'm going to take)

AMY: _____
(3. You're kidding./You kidded./Did you kid?)

Why _____ a rock to school?
(4. you're going to take/do you take/are you going to take)

RICK: Because _____ fossils in it.
(5. it's having/it has/it had)

AMY: _____ any fossils.
(6. I'm not seeing/I'm not going to see/I don't see)

RICK: Look here. _____ the leaf?
(7. Don't you see/Aren't you seeing/You're seeing)

AMY: Oh, yeah, and here are two snails.

RICK: _____ snails.
(8. Those didn't/Those aren't/Those are going to be)

_____ nautiluses.
(9. They're/Are they/They're going to be)

AMY: _____ a nautilus?
(10. What's/What do/What did)

RICK: _____ a sea animal.
(11. Is it/It does/It's)

_____ millions of years ago.
(12. This one probably lived/Did this one live/This one probably lives)

AMY: Where _____ the rock?
(13. did you find/you're finding/do you find)

RICK: _____ it.
(14. I don't find/I'm not finding/I didn't find)

_____ Joey's.
(15. It's going to be/it's/Was it)

_____ it to him last year.
(16. His father gave/His father gives/His father is giving)

_____ it.
(17. I just borrow/I just borrowed/Do I just borrow)

AMY: Why _____ it to school?
(18. are you going to take/do you take/did you take)

RICK: Because _____ fossils in Mr. Kenshaw's class.
(19. did we study/we're studying/we study)

_____ us some great fossils yesterday,
(20. He's showing/He showed/He shows)

but _____ as good as these.
(21. they weren't/they aren't going to be/aren't they)

AMY: _____ usually _____ fossils in biology?
(22. Do people ... study/Are people ... studying/Are people ... going to study)

RICK: Sure.

AMY: Well, when I was in high school, _____ them in
(23. we aren't studying/we don't study/we didn't study)

my class.

RICK: That's because _____ Mrs. Nelson.
(24. you had/you have/did you have)

_____ a very good teacher.
(25. She didn't/She isn't being/She's not)

AMY: Yes, _____!
(26. she is/she isn't/she does)

RICK: _____ with you now.
(27. I didn't argue/I'm not going to argue/Am I going to argue)

_____ too heavy. See you later.
(28. This rock is/This rock was/This rock is being)

Now you're ready for the computer. When you finish at the computer, go to page 102.

4 Complete the conversations. First change the question to a statement. (The statement will be an accusation.) Then look at the picture and write an appropriate short answer.

1. Did you forget the milk?
   BOB: *You forgot the milk.*
   ANN: *No, I didn't.* Look on the door.

2. Don't you have time for breakfast?
   ANN: *You don't have time for breakfast.*
   RICK: *Yes, I do.*

3. Doesn't your dog like me?
   DAN: _____
   BOB: _____ She just doesn't know you very well.

4. Did Jeff forget to call me?
   BOB: _____
   ANN: _____ He called when you were in the shower.

5. Aren't you going to finish in time?
   RICK: _____
   AMY: _____ The game doesn't start until 5:00.

6. Mom, is Amy breaking my truck?

RICK: Mom, _____

ANN: _____ She's fixing it.

7. Didn't Rick water the plants?

ANN: _____

BOB: _____ He just forgot that one.

8. Aren't the Pauleys going to take a vacation this year?

ANN: _____

BOB: _____ , but they're going to wait until October.

9. Isn't there any pie left?

RICK: _____

ANN: _____ Look on the second shelf.

10. Are you and Dad working too hard?

AMY: _____

ANN: _____ We're relaxing now.

103

5 Complete the conversation with the words in parentheses. Be sure to use the correct form and the correct tense of the verb.

RICK: *What are you doing?*
(1. what/you/do)

ANN: _____.
(2. I/read/an article/about amber)

RICK: Amber? _____?
(3. What/be/that)

ANN: _____.
(4. It/be/very old, very hard resin)

RICK: _____?
(5. What/be/resin)

ANN: _____. _____.
(6. It/be/a liquid) (7. You/find/it/in trees/like pine trees)

RICK: Oh.

ANN: Look. _____ of a piece
(8. Here/be/a picture)
of amber. _____.
(9. It/be/over 10,000 years old)

RICK: And _____!
(10. there/be/an insect/in it)

ANN: That's right. Thousands of years ago _____
_____. _____.
(11. that insect/walk/or fly/into the resin) (12. It/get stuck/and die)
Then _____.
(13. the resin/get/hard/and become amber)

RICK: It's beautiful.

ANN: _____. _____.
(14. I/know) (15. People/use/it/for jewelry/today)
_____ and all kinds of things from it.
(16. They/make/necklaces,/bracelets,)
See, _____. And _____?
(17. this man/make/a necklace) (18. you/see/this little round thing)

RICK: Yes.

ANN: _____.
(19. That/be/an air pocket)
_____.
(20. The air in that pocket/be/80 million years old)

104

RICK: _____! _____
(21. You/kid)   (22. There/be/dinosaurs on earth)
80 million years ago.

ANN: _____. And recently, _____
(23. I/know)   (24. some scientists/crush/a piece of amber)
_____ like this one, and _____.
(25. they/study/the air in the air pocket)

RICK: And _____?
(26. what/they/find)

ANN: _____
(27. They/find/that/the air 80 million years ago/have/50% more oxygen)
_____ than the air today.

RICK: Wow.

ANN: They say that in the future _____ in amber.
(28. they/study/more air pockets)

But _____.
(29. they/do (neg.)/it/right away)

First, _____. The ones they have now aren't very good.
(30. they/to make/better instruments)

RICK: _____. That old air could explain a lot of things.
(31. That/be/fabulous)

Like _____?
(32. why/the dinosaurs/die)

_____? _____?
(33. they/need/more oxygen/than we do)   (34. they/die/because/the air/lose oxygen)

ANN: Uh huh.

RICK: _____? _____?
(35. you/be/finished/with the article)   (36. I/can/read/it)

ANN: No, _____ with me.
(37. I/have/to take/it/to work)

But _____. I'll make one for you.
(38. I/make/several copies)

RICK: Thanks.